FOLK TALES FROM FRENCH LOUISIANA

RECORDED AND TRANSLATED

BY **Corinne L. Saucier**, PH. D.

Foreword by
IRENE WAGNER
Northwestern State College
Natchitoches, Louisiana

Baton Rouge
CLAITOR'S PUBLISHING DIVISION

FIRST EDITION

© 1962 by Louisiana State University. *All rights reserved, including the right of reproduction in whole or in part in any form, except for brief quotations in critical essays and reviews.* Manufactured in the United States of America.

Library of Congress catalog-card number: 62–13679

SECOND PRINTING, 1972
THIRD PRINTING, 1977
FOURTH PRINTING, 1981

ISBN No. 0-87511-100-9

CLAITOR'S PUBLISHING DIVISION

Published and for sale by:

CLAITOR'S PUBLISHING DIVISION
3165 S. Acadian at I-10, P.O. Box 3333
Baton Rouge, Louisiana 70821

FOLK TALES FROM
FRENCH LOUISIANA

By Dr. Saucier

History of Avoyelles Parish (1943)

Traditions de la Paroisse des Avoyelles en Louisiane (1956)

Histoire et Géographie des Avoyelles en Louisiane (1956)

Folk Tales From French Louisiana (1962)

To

our kind informants

who co-operated so happily

FOREWORD *

In Memoriam
CORINNE L[ELIA] SAUCIER
1890–1960

IN THE EARLY hours of February 1, 1960, Dr. Corinne L. Saucier departed this life at her home in Natchitoches, Louisiana. On February 9 she would have reached the age of seventy. Forty of those years had been spent in teaching in Louisiana—thirteen in the elementary schools, five as teacher of French in high schools, and twenty-four as teacher of French and Spanish at Northwestern State College, Natchitoches, from which position she had retired in 1955.

Miss Saucier's association with the Natchitoches campus actually began when, in her teens, she had come to the old Louisiana State Normal School to complete her high school credits and to obtain her teacher's diploma. Alternating between periods of study at the Normal and teaching in her native parish of Avoyelles, she obtained the diploma in 1914.

During years of serving as principal in West Baton Rouge and Pointe Coupee parishes, she attended three summer sessions at Louisiana State University. She then transferred her college credits to the George Peabody College for Teachers, which granted her B.S. degree in 1922 and her M.A. degree in August, 1923.

A French major, she chose as topic for her master's thesis "Louisiana Folk-tales and Songs in French Dialect, With Linguistic Notes." Her faculty advisers, impressed with her familiarity with her subject and the unique value of her collection of

* Reprinted, somewhat condensed, from *Louisiana Folklore Miscellany*, August, 1961.

American folklore, suggested that she continue her studies and eventually expand her findings into a doctoral dissertation. Thus began the project that was thenceforth to mark her as a student dedicated to research as well as to teaching. By the good fortune of French lineage and a French environment, she had all the tools to work with; and like her illustrious predecessor in the field of Louisiana folklore, Alcée Fortier, she had a passion for the French language and for preserving the traditions of the French people.

After receiving her master's degree, she taught French for several years at Alexandria. Then followed two years at the Sorbonne in Paris, where she received a diploma in June, 1929. Next, after a year and a half teaching French and Spanish at the College of St. Scholastica at Duluth, Minnesota, during which she attended one summer session at the University of Chicago, she entered Columbia University in 1930–31 with the intention of establishing residence for the eventual doctor's degree.

With this varied training and experience, Miss Saucier came to the Department of Modern Languages at the Louisiana State Normal College (now Northwestern State College) in 1931, where she was to spend the rest of her professional life. Now began what may be called the great stabilizing period of her life. The ceaseless struggle of earning in order to spend for more knowledge would ease with the increase of financial security, and life would be restored to a better balance. The doctorate had not yet been achieved, and adjustments would have to be made to new teaching skills, but she was again within the milieu of her folklore studies.

In the early thirties Miss Saucier was the first woman on the faculty to foresee the investment possibilities of owning real estate. She surprised her colleagues when, with keen business acumen, she bought a valuable lot directly across from the president's home on campus, on which she erected a substantial and attractive brick building, the first exclusively apartment house in Natchitoches. One of the apartments she retained as her home, and here through the years she extended hospitality to her friends and associates. She had great appreciation of home, her books, and the treasures collected in her travels. Gardening was one of her hobbies, and the flowers that bloomed in her yard were a great pleasure to her.*

Meanwhile, there was no lagging in efforts to improve her professional skills. In the summer of 1933 she spent two months perfecting her Spanish at the University of Mexico City, and she studied the history and literature of Colombia during a summer visit to Bogotá in 1939. One result of her Colombia trip was a bound typescript that she presented to Northwestern State College after her retirement—an anthology of selections from Colombian literature, designed especially for her Spanish classes. The variety of subjects in the selections depicts the life, customs, and thinking of the people; there are poems as well, and one short novel, along with biographical sketches of the authors and a glossary and conjugations.

Another by-product of this trip, an article entitled "My Summer in Bogotá, Colombia," appeared in the Peabody *Reflector* (August, 1940) and in the *Modern Language Journal* (January, 1941).

Northwestern State College has a second rare bound typescript volume of her textbook material, an anthology designed for reading in her French classes entitled "Anthology of Louisiana-French Literature," complete with biographical sketches of the authors, a glossary, and conjugations. The material is taken entirely from representative works of Louisiana-French writers, including some poems and songs (*chansons*), all chosen to show "local color and customs and at the same time to offer a variety of idioms for the second- and third-year student." This collection of classroom material is an incentive to the Louisiana student to appreciate his state's French background, and the Northwestern

---

* On March 30, 1962, under provisions of Dr. Saucier's will, the apartment building was transferred to Northwestern State College, with the provision that income from it be used for scholarships for needy young men and women from Avoyelles Parish. With other holdings the will also has established the Corinne Saucier Romance Language Scholarship Fund at Louisiana State University.

State College library considers it one of its most valuable Louisiana items.

During these busy years Miss Saucier never lost sight of the ultimate aim of her professional activity. In 1943 she published her first book, *History of Avoyelles Parish* (New Orleans). This comprehensive parish history, written in English, is really the steppingstone from which she moved off to a new start in her folklore research.

Three years later, in June and July of 1946, she attended Laval University in Quebec, and here at last found the environment best suited for her gráduate study. On leave of absence from Northwestern State, she returned to Laval in the spring of 1948 to pursue work for her doctorate; and there, after having taken a few months to enlarge her collection of folklore in Louisiana, she was granted the degree Doctor of Philosophy in August, 1949. Her dissertation was "Histoire et traditions de la paroisse des Avoyelles in Louisiane."

She returned to her duties at Northwestern State looking forward to increased activity in publication, but the years of concentration and tremendous effort had takৎ a heavy toll of her strength. In the spring of 1951 she suffered her first heart attack. Although forced to husband her physical resources, her mind and spirit felt no diminution of strength, and she continued to meet her classes and planned the publication of her dissertation in four volumes. *Histoire et géographie des Avoyelles en Louisiane* was published in New Orleans in 1956, and *Traditions de la paroisse des Avoyelles en Louisiane* appeared as Volume 47 of the *Memoirs of the American Folk-Lore Society* (1956). Then followed delay and complications in publication of the two final volumes, the heart of the research. Yielding to her publisher's request to present the folk tales in English, she underwent the labor of preparing translations during her last few months. The fourth volume, an impressive collection of seventy-one songs (children's, love, military, and religious songs as well as ballads, rondels, and medleys) has not yet been published.

Dr. Saucier's last public-program appearance was made on

April 19, 1958, when she addressed the state meeting of the Louisiana Folklore Society on Northwestern's campus. In her address, "The Ups and Downs of Collecting Folklore in Avoyelles Parish," she described her experiences in collecting the tales and songs of the third and fourth volumes of her dissertation. She spoke of the complications that had arisen: ". . . so many," she added, "that I am getting weary of it—especially when I think of the sad side of my work: most of my contributors have passed away since that eventful year for me 1949." However much she realized that her own strength was waning, she closed on a hopeful note: the gathering of folk literature is not finished; the young blood in the young society will furnish the life to carry on.

Dr. Saucier engaged in many professional activities. On the local campus she was a member of the American Association of University Women, the American Association of University Professors, and Delta Kappa Gamma—for the last of which she served as treasurer, 1943–45, and wrote a number of biographies that went into *Pioneer Women Teachers of Louisiana,* published in 1954 by Epsilon Organization, Delta Kappa Gamma. She had served as vice-president of the Modern Language Section of the Louisiana Teachers Association, before which she had read papers; and in 1951 she was chairman of the Classical and Foreign Language Section of the Louisiana College Conference. She was a member of the Modern Language Association and attended many of its national conventions.

In the American Folk-Lore Society, of which she was a member, she attained national distinction as a specialist in Louisiana folklore, and she presented a paper before its national convention at El Paso, Texas, December 23, 1952.

In a very real sense, Dr. Corinne L. Saucier was an educator. With absolute independence of spirit she followed one goal in life—education. In attaining this goal, she was dominated by one ideal: that of unswerving loyalty to those simple virtues that are basic to native culture and that, as such, are the foundation upon which education is to be built. Her greatest service to education lies in the fact that she brought to the youth of Louisiana a new respect and appreciation for all that was fine in their native background.

In death she was returned to the parish that she had so honored in life. She lies by the side of her parents in the cemetery at Marksville, Louisiana.

IRENE WAGNER

Northwestern State College
Natchitoches, Louisiana

CONTENTS

THE INFORMANTS from whom these stories were collected are listed after the titles below. Variants reprinted from other sources are numbered 22*a*, 24*a–b*, 33*a*. (Other published variants are listed in Appendix B.)

III. COMICAL TALES

IV. ANIMAL TALES

APPENDIXES

INTRODUCTION

THIS SMALL VOLUME of folk tales is divided into four categories; semi-legendary, fairy, comical, and animal stories. These tales were collected from French-speaking raconteurs in Avoyelles Parish, Louisiana. Those collected in 1923 were dictated to the writer by a person who could read and speak both French and English. The collection made in 1949 was more comprehensive. Several raconteurs from different parts of the parish contributed. Records were made of these tales and furnish an excellent source for study of the spoken French of central Louisiana.

It is with this thought in mind that the author wrote "Histoire et traditions de la paroisse des Avoyelles en Louisiane" under the direction of Professor Luc Lacourcière at Laval University, Quebec, Canada, in 1949. This piece of research is divided into four chapters: (1) "Histoire de la paroisse des Avoyelles," (2) "Les mœurs," (3) "Les traditions orales," (4) "La langue." Because the dissertation is rather voluminous, it was decided to make four volumes of it. The first one is entitled *Histoire et géographie des Avoyelles en Louisiane,* the text of which is a translation in condensed form of the English version written and copyrighted in 1943 by the author, and was published by the Pelican Publishing Company of New Orleans, Louisiana, in 1956; the second volume was also published in 1956, by the American Folk-Lore Society of Philadelphia, Pennsylvania. It is entitled *Traditions de la paroisse des Avoyelles en Louisiane.* This volume is the third in the series and is part of Chapter Three. It was intended to be bilingual but because of publication problems the plan was changed. The first part of Chapter Three was included in the second volume, while the last part of it is to be volume four entitled *Romancero de la Louisiane: Folksongs,* to be published later.

The author feels indebted to many persons who were kind enough to give their time and interest in order to make this work possible, too many to enumerate here. However, the names of the raconteurs are listed in the Contents with a few data showing that they have either passed away or have reached a "ripe old age," proving the importance of collecting these tales before they are lost forever.

Our folk tales were brought to Louisiana by the early colonists who came from France and from Canada. This can be seen by consulting the works of Sébillot, authority on French folklore, and the collection made by M. Marius Barbeau in the Province of Quebec and published in volumes 29, 30, 32, 36, 39, 44 and 53 of *The Journal of American Folk-Lore*.

Just as the language has changed, so have the folk tales. We find that in some cases only fragments of the original stories have been retained. Tom Thumb (*Poucette*) and *Minette et ses roulettes* are two very good examples of this phenomenon. For this reason we give variants of Alcée Fortier's folk tales showing how these changes occur in one's lifetime. Variants of animal tales can be found in Part II (1936) of Elsie Clews Parsons' *Folk-Lore of the Antilles, French and English*, published in three parts as Volume 26 of the *Memoirs of the American Folk-Lore Society*.

As stated above, our collection of folk tales was made in Avoyelles Parish, which is in central Louisiana, but these stories were heard all over southern Louisiana until modern times changed the favorite form of entertainment from storytelling and folk singing to listening to radio and to watching television of our day. Our raconteurs, or storytellers, listed in this volume are all of the horse-and-buggy days. They all learned their art from their mothers or another member of the family— showing that it was a family form of entertainment. Naturally it was more popular in rural areas.

Much can be learned about local speech and local customs from these stories, for they vary from place to place and with the passing of time. Since our collection of 1949 was made by means of an electric recorder, we have an excellent source to study local pronunciation as well as the morphology of the French language as spoken today. Unfortunately that part of our research had to be omitted from this volume. We simply translated the stories from French to English, leaving out the complicated angle of linguistics.

We realize that folklore is international and timeless. It has existed throughout the centuries; it is as ageless as humanity because it reflects life in all its manifestations even though at times it seems farfetched and unreal. In fact, our collection is a proof that fairy tales are the favorite type, because they out-number the other types listed here.

'Tit Jean, or Little John, is a special favorite. He appears in different roles but is principally the defender of princesses and fighter of giants, etc. Foolish John is about as stupid as one can imagine. The name has become a byword in everyday language. For the same reason, Roclore has become a byword for a ruse type of person. Jean Malin is the cunning type.

We regret that our collection of animal stories is so limited after having included a few in another volume, but there are enough to appreciate their similarity to those collected by Alcée Fortier, and to the fabliaux of early French literature. There is definitely a note of realism here in contrast to the fairy tales with their setting in a world of fantasy. We are pleased to have a fairly large variety of stories, representative, if not all-inclusive, of our southern Louisiana form of oral literature known as folk-lore, a heritage that is disappearing in our mechanized age.

C. S.

FOLK TALES FROM
FRENCH LOUISIANA

I. SEMI-LEGENDARY

1

GENEVIÈVE DE BRABANT

This story was used in art and architecture in the eighteenth century. Encyclopaedia Britannica, *Volume X (Chicago, 1948), page 115, has this to say*:

Geneviève, Genoveva or Genovefa of Brabant figured in medieval legends. Her story is a typical example of the widespread talk of the chaste wife falsely accused and repudiated, generally on the word of a rejected suitor. She was said to be the wife of the palatine Siegfried of Treves and was falsely accused by the major-domo, Golo. Sentenced to death she was spared by the executioner and lived six years with her son in a cave in the Ardennes, nourished by a roe. Siegfried, who had meanwhile found out Golo's treachery, was chasing the roe when he discovered her hiding place and reinstated her in her former honour. Her story is said to rest on the history of Marie of Brabant, wife of Louis IV, Duke of Bavaria and Count Palatine of the Rhine, who was tried by her husband and beheaded on the 18th of January, 1256, for supposed infidelity. A crime for which Louis afterwards had to do penance. The change in name may be due to the cult of St. Geneviève, patroness of Paris. The tale first obtained wide popularity in L'innocence reconnue; ou, Vie de Sainte-Geneviève de Brabant, printed in 1638 by the Jesuit René de Cerisier (1603–1662) and a frequent subject for dramatic representation in Germany.

According to La Rousse Pourtous, *the first writer to use this subject was Jacques de Voragine in the thirteenth century. It was a popular subject all over Europe.*

COME, ALL YOU WHO WISH to hear the story of Geneviève de Brabant! She was married to a nobleman. War was declared and her husband had to go and fight for his country. He left her in the care of a brutal king named Golo who tried to seduce her. When she discouraged his advances, he had her put in jail. There she gave birth to a son whom she called Belani. When the child was two years old, Golo ordered four of his valets to take her and her child to the forest, kill them, and bring him her tongue as proof that they had obeyed his order.

The two valets went with her deep in the forest and stopped for a discussion. She said to them: "If you wish to please me, kill my child before you do me." The two valets looked at each other. One of them said: "Why should we kill our mistress who has never done us any harm?" The other responded: "I know how we can deceive Golo—we shall kill the little dog that followed us and bring Golo the dog's tongue." He then turned to Geneviève and said: "Go, woman, into the forest, and never leave it, for if you are ever seen alive, Golo will have us executed and our bodies thrown into the gutters."

The woman promised to remain in the woods, and she did. Several days later, a roe came to them to nurse the child. Geneviève herself ate only wild fruits and the vegetation she found in the woods. Every day she would go in swimming in a small lake and would say to her son: "If you are ever called to the castle, you will be recognized because of the striking resemblance you bear to your father."

War finally came to an end. Her husband returned. He went to see Golo, who told him that his wife and child had died. He was grief-stricken. To kill time, he would go into the woods to hunt and fish.

One day on a hunting trip, his hunting dogs startled the roe that was nursing Geneviève's child. She immediately went to Geneviève, and the hunting dogs stopped when they saw that woman in the woods. Soon her husband arrived. He said to her: "Woman, what are you doing here in the forest? Tell me your name." "My name," she said to him, "is Geneviève, born in Brabant. I was married to a nobleman. My husband had to go to war. He left me in the care of a king who wished to seduce me; who had four valets take me into the forest to kill me, but they felt sorry for me and did not carry out the king's order. I was left here in the woods, where I have been ever since."

Her husband was so happy to have found her, he threw his coat around her shoulders, he lifted her and the child that he adored, and took them to his castle. But she, having lived so long in the wilderness on uncooked food, could not adjust to the change. She wasted away and died. The roe, which had been brought with them, would neither eat nor drink. She would lie on Geneviève's grave, and there she died of grief. Then poor Belani, beside himself with grief, would weep and sob and roll on the ground. And the poor king, feeling guilty, wept bitterly. And that is the end. Geneviève's husband had Golo executed and torn to pieces and thrown in the gutters.

II. FAIRY TALES

2

CINDERELLA

ONCE UPON A TIME a widow married a widower. She had two daughters and her husband had one whose name was Cinderella. She sat in a corner by the fire and spent her time playing in the ashes, for she was never allowed to go anywhere with the family.

One day there was a big dance in town. Of course Cinderella could not go, because she did not have good clothes, but her two stepsisters went. When they returned, they told her what beautiful things they had seen and heard—music, dancing and the prince—how handsome he was! "Oh well," she said, "I am as beautiful as any of those girls." The sisters answered: "You are a fine one, in the ashes all the time. What would you look like among all those beautiful girls?"

Well, there came to Cinderella what is called a magician. He said to her: "Do you wish to go to the ball?" She replied: "I would like nothing better, but I do not have anything to wear." "Well," he said, "I can get you everything you need." He struck his wand on the hearth and said: "By virtue of my little wand, I wish Cinderella to have beautiful clothes, a coach, four horses and a coachman to take her to the dance." Immediately there appeared a beautiful outfit including four white horses, a coach and a coachman. Cinderella was ready to go, but the magician warned her to return before eleven o'clock else she would revert to her natural self.

At the ball, Cinderella was the main attraction. The prince wanted every dance with her. He was with her constantly. A little before eleven she said she just had to go home. All the guests begged her to stay, but she ran out to her coach and left. At home when the sisters returned they exclaimed: "Cinderella, if you could have seen the beautiful princess at the ball! She was the belle of the ball." "Well," she replied, "she was not more beautiful than I." "Well," they responded, "you should be ashamed of yourself to speak that way." She remarked: "She is not more beautiful than I."

So the prince said he would give another ball to find out where the beautiful princess lived. As before, the stepsisters went, but not Cinderella. Again, the magician came to her and asked her if she wanted to go. She replied that she did. Striking his wand on the hearth, he said: "By the virtue of my little wand may Cinderella have her coach and coachman." She wore silver slippers. At the ball the prince met her at the door and danced with her the whole evening. At eleven, she said that she had to go home. He insisted on her staying, but she ran out so fast that one of her slippers came off. The prince picked it up and kept it.

The next day he went from house to house looking for the girl who could wear the slipper. At Cinderella's home, of course, her stepsisters tried very hard to have it fit, but it was too small. At that moment he saw Cinderella and suggested that she try it on. They exclaimed: "Oh, she is just Cinderella and could never wear it; besides, she was not at the dance." Then Cinderella tried it on and it was just her fit.

"Well," he said, "this is the young lady who was at the ball." Then she admitted that she had gone to the ball both nights; she was the beautiful princess. The prince took her home and married her. Her stepsisters were very jealous of her.

3

JULIE AND JULIEN
OR
BLUE BEARD

ONCE UPON A TIME there was a young man who was a good gambler. He would gamble everything he had. One day, on his way to a gambling place, he stopped at a saloon. There he met Blue Beard, with whom he undertook to play cards. Blue Beard won every time, getting all his earthly belongings, including his horse tied at the gate; then he bet a year's work, which Blue Beard won also.

When the game was over, Blue Beard said to the young man: "I give you three weeks to find out where I live, to come and start your year's work. If you cannot find it, you will be destroyed." The young man was very worried. He went to spend the night with his grandmother, who was a sorceress. She knew the future and everything that happened. She said to him: "Go, and speak to the old woman who lives on the river bank at a particular spot. She speaks with all flying creatures. Perhaps she knows where Blue Beard lives."

So he went and asked her if it was true. She answered it was true that she spoke with all creatures that could talk. She said: "I am going to call all of them and ask them." She did, and finally an old eagle came and answered: "I passed by his house only yesterday. He lives on an island where no one ever goes." He asked the eagle: "Could you take me there?"

And so he left, the eagle leading him. When they reached Blue Beard's home, the eagle said to the young man: "He has three daughters who have never seen a man. They will find it very strange." The young man kept going and entered the yard which had many shrubs and flowers. He hid among them and waited. Every afternoon at four, the young ladies would gather some of the flowers. As usual, that afternoon, they went out to get flowers. They found the young man, whose name was Julien. The youngest daughter's name was Julie. They invited Julien into the house and told their mother they had found a little old man. He sat on the porch with the young ladies.

That night when Blue Beard came home, Julien asked him: "What task am I assigned for tomorrow?" Blue Beard took him to a bayou, gave him a leaking basket and a thimble and said to him: "You will have to empty this arm of the sea with this basket or I shall kill you tonight." The man began to cry.

Julie, the youngest daughter, said: "I am going to carry the hired man's lunch to him." So she went and said to Julien: "Don't cry, don't cry. I can make you succeed. Listen to me. Here is a little wand, and at four this afternoon, say: 'By the virtue of this little wand, may this arm of the sea be dry when Blue Beard gets here!' Go down and get him the last drop and throw it at his feet."

And so he did as he was told. That night when Blue Beard returned, the task had been performed, so he took Julien home again. The next morning when he was asked what Julien was to do that day, he was told that he had to clear the wooded area nearby with a wooden ax, or lose his life.

Again, Julien began weeping and again, Julie went to him with his lunch. She was very much in love with him by now and assured him she could help him out of his predicament. She said: "Don't cry. At four o'clock this afternoon, wish that this wooded island be cleared and only one piece of wood left. When Father comes tonight, grab it and throw it on the piled wood, and everything will be all right." Julien did as he was told. When he saw Blue Beard coming, he grabbed the last piece of wood and threw it on the pile. Blue Beard said to him: "Come, your day's work is done." So that night, Julie said to him: "We shall have to leave. Papa is going to kill you. I shall treat three pins and place them on a cork stopper which I shall put on the mantel. The pins will answer for us."

The old man and his wife were suspicious. They l l an idea

Julie and Julien were planning to elope. During the night, the old woman called her husband and said to him: "Listen, Julie and Julien are gone, I tell you." He replied: "No." She asked him to call them and see. He did, and the pin answered: "Yes, Father." He turned to her and said: "I told you so. They are not going to leave."

A little later the old woman repeated: "They have gone, I tell you." The old man called: "Julie and Julien." The second pin answered: "What do you want, Father?" Then he said to her: "I tell you they are not going to leave." But the old woman was very much worried about her daughter and called: "Julie and Julien," and once more the reply came: "What is it, Father?" "Well," he said, "you will let me alone now."

But in spite of it all, the old woman was worried and she kept after her husband to call again. This he did finally, but there was no answer now, no more magic pins. "Well," he said, "they have left, but I shall overtake them tomorrow morning!"

So early the next morning he left. In the meantime, Julie said to Julien: "If you see anything unusual, tell me. Papa is coming to get us. We shall have to throw him off the track by assuming different forms." Just then he said to her: "I see a man coming on a terrible horse, something like a cloud." "Well," she said, "it is my father. Let's turn into two little pigs in these briars." They did. Old Blue Beard came. He tried hard to catch them, but could not. So he went home. His wife asked him if he had seen anything. He replied that he had seen two lean pigs. "Well," she said, "it was they. Why did you not catch them?" He promised to try again the next day.

All this time, Julie and Julien kept going. She said to him: "If you see the horse in a cloud, tell me. It will be my father coming to get us." A short while later, he exclaimed: "I see him!" They were near an old church. She decided for them to be two altar boys and to answer to anything asked them: *Bobinus bobiscum* (*Dominus vobiscum*—The Lord be with you). So they became two altar boys at the foot of the altar. The old man appeared at the door and asked if they had seen a man and a woman go by. They answered him: *"Bobinus bobiscum."* "That

is not what I ask," he said. "Have you seen a man and a woman
go by?" To everything, the altar boys answered: "*Bobinus
bobiscum,*" so he gave up and went home. His wife wanted to
know what he had seen. He related his experience and she
assured him that the altar boys were Julie and Julien and that
he should have brought them home. She said: "Tomorrow, I
shall go." And so she did.

Julie said to her husband: "Today, Mamma will come. It
will be a yellow cloud and a horse this time. You must tell me
if you see her." "Well, I see her at this very moment," he exclaimed. They were near a river. They turned into two little
ducks on the river, but the old woman knew who they were. She
was a sorceress. She went to the edge of the water and called and
called. The drake would turn to go to her, but the little female
would head him off. This went on all afternoon. So the old woman
gave up with these words: "Go, Julie and Julien, we shall never
come back for you."

They crossed the river and built a small house on the bank.
They had been there about six months when Julien asked Julie
to let him go see his parents. He was homesick. She answered no,
because they would kiss him and that would make him forget
her. Finally she granted him the permission to go, if he promised
to kiss no one.

So Julien left, and after a long, hard trip on foot, he arrived
at his parents' home, tired and exhausted. They wished to
kiss him, but he pushed them away saying he was married to
a very bright girl who had asked him to kiss no one, for that
would make him forget her.

So he lay down at his mother's feet. She was so happy and
proud of him, she fanned the flies away from him. He went to
sleep and while he was asleep, she stooped and kissed him out
of joy at seeing her son whom she had not seen in so many
years. When he awoke he could remember nothing at all. Several
days later, his mother asked him: "Why don't you go get your
wife? You told us you were married." He replied: "Did I tell
you that? I do not remember a thing." They assured him that
he had told them that he was married to a bright woman. So

they let him alone. Sometime later, Julien started dating a young woman and he made plans to marry her.

A hunter had passed by the home of a widow living on the bank of a river. She was so bright that he asked permission of the bride's parents to allow the widow to make a speech at the wedding, when every guest would be asked to do so. The parents of the bride readily consented and the hunter went to see the widow, who agreed to attend the wedding provided she would be allowed to make her hen and rooster talk. They agreed, even said they would be most happy to have this entertainment. So she went to the wedding. All the guests were making speeches. Julien was seated at the table. When it came to the widow's turn, she put her hen and her rooster on the table and threw a grain of corn between them.

The rooster ate the corn and the hen said to him: "You are a fine one." He asked: "How is that?" She replied: "You remember nothing of all that I did for you. I saved your life three times, and when you left home to go see your parents, I pleaded with you not to kiss anyone because you would forget me if you did so. It was not you, but your mother who kissed you, and you have forgotten me."

Suddenly, Julien remembered all. He recognized his wife. He went up to the bride's father and asked: "If you had lost a key and went to buy another and on your way you found the old one, which one would you use?" "Well," the father answered, "I would use the old one." "Well then," said Julien, "here is your daughter and I shall take back my wife."

4

THE SEVEN-HEADED ANIMAL
OR
FEARLESS JOHN

ONCE UPON A TIME a man and a woman, although married for twenty years, had no children. One morning upon arising, they found an infant well wrapped near the well. He was a very beautiful child. The man was very proud of this foundling. After a few years he noticed the boy was not afraid of anything. He said to his lady: "We shall call him Fearless John." When the boy was eighteen years old, he asked his father what fear was. The father said: "It is a terrible feeling. It paralyzes one's movements." "Well," said the boy, "I must find out what fear is. I am going away."

So he left and on his way he met an old Baptist minister. John asked him to explain fear to him. The old minister told him to go into the old church nearby that night and listen to the noise there. He would then experience the emotion of fear.

John did as he was told and heard the noise, but he chased it outside into the cemetery. The next morning, he went to the old priest's home and asked for his spade. He wanted to dig into the graves of those who had tried to frighten him the night before. The old priest said: "Let them alone. I shall give you ten dollars to let them alone and leave the place."

So John left and walked on until he came to a wooded area. There he saw a bear, a lion, and a tiger eating a man. John was carrying a sword with which he cut the corpse into three parts, giving each animal his share. He walked on, and after while he turned around and noticed the animals were following him. He said to them: "So you are not satisfied with one body, you want another." "Well," they answered, "you helped us out once; we

wish to return the good deed if the occasion arises." "Fine," said
John, "let's go."

He continued his quest for fear. One day he went to the edge
of a town and noticed it was decorated in white. He asked why
so much white. He was told that every year the seven-headed
animal devoured a fifteen-year-old maiden. This year, the
king's daughter had been chosen and he had ordered the white
decoration.

"Well," he cried, "I want to see this affair." "Oh," they replied,
"do not go near the gallows. The seven-headed beast will eat
you too." He had taken very good care of his three animals.
They were strong and fat. He went to the stand and sat down
with the animals by him. The young lady was seated nearby
in a beautiful chair, ready for the sacrifice. After a while he
heard a terrible noise. He looked and saw the seven-headed
beast coming to devour the young lady. He said to his animals:
"Leave me." He drew his sword while his animals held the
beast and bit it as hard as they could. He then slew the beast
by cutting off the seven heads, thus saving the girl's life. She
said to him: "I will never marry another man but you. You
have saved my life." "Well," he answered, "I have to find fear.
I will return in a year and a day, and will marry you then."

The next morning, a man named Grand Vizier passed by and
saw that the beast had been killed. He was riding in a wagon.
He picked up the seven heads and went to the king's palace,
telling the king that he had killed it and that he wanted to marry
his daughter. The king gave him permission to do so, but the
princess said she did not wish to marry before a year and a day.

So after a year and a day, preparations for the wedding were
begun. Fearless John arrived and stationed himself on the edge
of the town, where he learned that the Grand Vizier was planning
to marry the princess. John wrote a note to the princess, hung
it around the bear's neck and told him to go to the princess
with the note for a bottle of wine and a capon for a meal. The
bear went. The watchman wanted to kill him, but the king said
that the day was an exceptional one and the animal's life would
be spared. The bear went to the princess and rubbed against

her knees. She saw the note around his neck, read it, placed the articles asked for in a large towel, and the bear went back to John. Then he told his lion to go get him the best suit of clothes in town. The lion went to the palace carrying around his neck a small card. He rubbed against the girl's knees and she saw the card, read it and sent the best suit in town. The lion went back to Fearless John.

He dressed and went to the palace where the wedding was taking place. He said to the king: "Who do you believe killed the seven-headed animal—he who can show you the seven heads, or he who can show you the seven tongues in a handkerchief here in your home?" "Oh," replied the king, "the one with the handkerchief." "Well, here it is," he said. He had taken the seven tongues. He pulled out the handkerchief as proof, and also showed pearls hung around his animals' necks at the gallows. The princess got up at this moment and said they had killed the beast and that she would marry no one else but Fearless John. So they were married and the Grand Vizier was hanged.

5

BEAUTY AND THE BEAST

ONCE UPON A TIME there was a man who had three daughters, the eldest of whom was poorly treated. The other daughters thought they were superior to her. One day their father went to town. The younger daughters asked him to bring them two beautiful dresses; then he went to the eldest and in a very rough manner asked her what she wanted. She answered that she wanted the most beautiful rose he would see. To this he said: "All right."

The father went to town, and returning he passed by a beautiful unoccupied house around which there was a beautiful flower garden. The roses reminded him of his daughter's wish.

He got out and went into the garden to pick a rose. There came to him a large and fat black beast that asked him what he wanted to do with that rose. He replied that it was to please his daughter. "Well," said the beast, "you may have it, but your daughter will have to come and sleep alone in this house tonight if she wants the rose."

So he went home, gave his daughter the rose and told her the story. "Well," she replied, "as long as I am so unhappy here, I had just as well try this experiment." So he took her to the big house. She sat down in a chair in the dark. After her father left, the fat beast appeared and went around her chair, not saying a word.

A while later she started crying. The beast returned and walked around the chair again and then retired to the rear of the house. All was quiet for a while. Then she heard groans in the rear, very mournful sounds, and she decided to investigate at the risk of being killed.

She advanced toward the source of the plaints until she got to the spot and asked for help because she was dying from fright. She heard a human voice. It was a prince in a bear's skin. He said: "This was a test to see if you loved me enough to stand it." He was the king's son, a prince. He married her and she was now richer than any of them.

He said to her: "The rose which you have there, that I gave you, is a magic rose. Whenever you wish to go to your father's, just hold the rose in your hand and say: 'I wish to be at Father's,' and you will be there immediately without walking. Do likewise to return, and whatever you wish the rest of your days, you can have."

6

THE TURKEY RAISER

ONCE UPON A TIME there was a man who had a son. When the son reached a certain age, he asked his father to tell him who his godfather was. "Well," answered the father, "I cannot tell you. You sit on the gatepost and say to every passer-by, 'good day, Godfather,' and he who truly is your godfather will say, 'good day, Godchild.'"

So the next morning early, he climbed to the top of the gatepost and said to every passer-by: "Good day, Godfather." "I am not your godfather," replied the first passer-by. This went on until ten o'clock when a passer-by, on a large black horse, said: "Good day, Godchild. Get on my horse behind me, since you are my godchild." He climbed on and discovered he was riding with the devil.

He rode far away. The devil opened the house and said: "Since you are my godchild, I shall give you my keys. You may go into six rooms, but not into the seventh. If you open it, I shall know it and I will kill you. I do not live here."

After he left, the godchild went into the first room and saw a horse and a trough filled with meat. He opened the second room and saw a lion and a trough filled with oats. "Oh," he said, "godfather is too stupid. I shall place the oats in the horse's trough and the meat in the lion's trough."

The horse thanked him heartily for this kind deed. The young man continued the round of rooms. He entered the third room, then the fourth, the fifth and the sixth, in all of which he saw parts of the human body. Then he decided he wanted to see the seventh. So he opened it and assured himself that his godfather would never know it. But a drop of gold fell on his hair as soon as he entered the forbidden room. He began to weep and said: "When Godfather comes, he will know that I opened the seventh room." He went to the first room where he had seen the horse. The horse wanted to know why he was crying. He told the horse the whole story and was told not to cry. There was a way out, but he must follow directions if he wished to save his life.

The young man asked for the directions. The horse answered: "Get on my back and ride me as hard as you can; then, when I am exhausted, get off, gather as much of my sweat as possible and put it in a small bottle. When your godfather comes for you, throw the bottle against a tree to break it. A river will form, which he will never be able to cross." So the young man did as he was told. When the horse was very tired, he got off and filled the small bottle with sweat. The horse said to him: "Pull out three hairs from my tail, and when you will be in deep trouble, say: 'Come to my aid, my horse,' and I shall be there instantly. Never remove the hairs from your pocket." So the young man did as he was told.

Soon after the horse left, the godfather appeared. The young man crushed the bottle against a tree and a veritable sea began to flow around. The godfather could not cross it. The young man kept on walking, and soon he came to the king's palace. He asked for work. The king gave him the job of tending his turkeys. The young man was happy in his work, especially when he met the king's pretty daughter.

A man named Grand Vizier was courting her. One of the servants told her one day that she would never marry Grand Vizier if she could see the turkey raiser. "He is bright, he is handsome with hair of pure gold, and he speaks very well indeed." "Well," said the young lady, "tell him to come to my room. I wish to speak to him." He replied: "I cannot, unless I have a good suit of clothes." "Well," she said to her servant, "take him this money and tell him to buy a suit. I want him to come and converse with me."

He went and bought a nice suit. He dressed up and went to see the princess. She found him wonderful. He suited her exactly. But her lover, the Grand Vizier, got very jealous. He understood that the king's daughter preferred the turkey raiser to him. So he planned a way to get rid of him. He told her that the young man was bragging about going to get the golden-haired beauty living in a small chateau on an arm of the sea and bringing her for their wedding.

He called the turkey raiser and asked him if it was true he was bragging about such a feat. The young man answered: "I cannot do such a thing." But the jealous man said he had to go or he would lose his life. He had to come across. So the young man left, crying, knowing he could never perform the task. When he reached the river bank, he thought of his horse and said: "My horse, come to me." The horse appeared at his side asking: "What do you want?"

He told the horse the whole story. The horse told him to go to the small house where there were many giants who were very strong. "Give them whiskey, and when they are tipsy, rent a boat and tell them you wager they cannot place Golden Hair's chateau on the boat, and when they do so, an easy thing for them, shove off and come to the king's palace."

So he did what the horse had told him to do. He got the giants tipsy, then got them to load the house on the deck of the boat, and they shoved off into the water. The golden-haired beauty was worried to death. She had a large trunk in which were all her jewels. She said: "I do not want anyone to get my jewels. I am going to throw my keys into the sea." She did so, and soon was at the king's palace. He went to meet her and asked her how she liked the place. She answered: "I would like it better if I had my keys. This morning, I was so upset that I threw my keys into the sea. All my things are in my trunk which is locked."

The Grand Vizier saw another chance to get rid of his rival, so he told the king that the young man was anxious to go get the keys. Again, the turkey raiser explained that he could not perform such a task, but the king threatened to destroy him if he did not do it. So the young man left. He thought of his horse and pulled out the second hair from his pocket and said: "Come to me, my horse." Again, the horse appeared and asked what he wanted. He told him. The horse advised him to go back to "where you got the boat. You will find a sailor woman there who

is half-fish and half-human. She can talk with all the fish in the
sea. Ask her to ask the fish if they have not seen the keys. They
will get them for you."

He did as he was told. He asked the lady sailor and she said
that she did know all the fish. She called all of them. The last one
was a bream (patassa). He said that he had just seen the keys
hanging on a rock, not touching the ground. "Could you go get
them?" she asked. "Oh yes. The man can go to bed and sleep
tonight. I will be here with them tomorrow morning," he replied.

So he went and the young man went to bed and slept. At
dawn, the patassa was on the shore with the keys hanging on
his fins. The young man got them and rushed to the king's
palace with them. When the young girl saw what was taking
place, she said to her father: "All these tricks of Grand Vizier's
are useless. He wants to get rid of the young turkey raiser, but
I will never marry anyone else. You can do what you please, I
shall never marry anyone else."

The king hanged Grand Vizier at the end of the table. The
young man was now very happy, for he had married the princess.
He thought of his horse and pulled out of his pocket the third
and last hair and exclaimed: "My horse, come to me." The
horse appeared and neighed loudly. Suddenly, he turned into
a man who had been enchanted by the devil. There was a happy
reunion with his wife, the golden-haired beauty brought there
by the young man, soon to be a king.

7

THE RISING WATER, THE TALKING BIRD AND THE WEEPING TREE

ONCE UPON A TIME there were three sisters who lived on the king's estate. One night, while the Grand Vizier was passing by, one of them said to her sisters: "It is time we made the mush for supper." Another sister said: "I wish I were the baker's wife; then I would have bread to eat." Then the second one exclaimed: "In this wishing game, I wish I were the cook's wife." "Well," added the third one, "I wish I were the king's wife; then I would have everything."

Grand Vizier went to the king with this story, who told him to bring the three sisters to him. They came, fearing they were going to be accused of some crime. The king asked which one wished to marry the baker. They were afraid to say. Finally one spoke and said: "I did." "Well," the king answered, "you will be the baker's wife. Now, which one wanted to be the cook's wife?" The second sister said: "I did." He answered that she would be the cook's wife. Then came the third question. "Which one wants to be the king's wife?" The third sister said: "I do." "Well," he answered, "I am the king and you will be my wife."

A few years later the people of the kingdom got very jealous of the poor girl who had married the king. So they gossiped. When the king's first child came, the rumors were that it was afflicted, that it looked like a dog, that it was stillborn. It was given to the Grand Vizier to rear. The king was very much disappointed. The same thing happened for the second child, a girl. She, too, was given to the Grand Vizier. The story was repeated when the third child, a girl, was born. They said it looked like a cat. The king then said: "I do not want such a wife."

He put her in a small tent just outside the gate and let the passers-by slap her and spit in her face.

Years later the king was hunting in the woods. He met a fine-looking boy—a young man—and said to him: "I am so glad to meet you. I did not expect to meet such a fine man. Where do you live?" The young man answered: "Here in the kingdom."

This boy, or young man, had heard of a place called Rising Water, Talking Bird, and the Weeping Tree. He said: "I am going to try to find it." His sisters said: "Don't do this. You know how many have been turned into stone on the way to find such things. We shall never see you again." He answered: "I promise you I will return." Everyone who tried to find this place failed. They did not do what was necessary to get the wanted results.

So he went, taking his bucket. He dipped his bucket in the water, filling it; then he threw water on each of the stone statues. Immediately they became the human beings they had been before. But he was called on all sides, in an effort to make him turn around, thereby making him turn into stone. He had what he set out to get: Rising Water, Talking Bird, and Weeping Tree. He took them home. The next day he went hunting again and saw the king once more. They were happy to see each other. The young man told the king he had two sisters at home. The king expressed a wish to see them. He was invited for dinner the next day. When the young man got home he told his sisters to prepare dinner for the king. The talking bird said to prepare stuffed cucumbers with pearls. So the sisters prepared this dish and others.

When the king arrived for dinner, he met the two young ladies. He thought they were fine. Dinner was served and when the cucumbers were passed around, the king wanted to know "why stuff cucumbers with pearls?" "Well," the talking bird answered: "It isn't any stranger than your thinking that your children were puppies and kittens and everything else. Here is your family."

8

THE MAN AND HIS SON

ONCE UPON A TIME a man had an only child, who was very bright. The devil taught school about a mile from the home of this old man. The little boy attended this school. He was so bright that he could become anything he wanted. He had learned this art from the devil. The boy told his father that the devil wanted him because he realized how bright he was, even brighter than his teacher. He said to his father: "If you just listen to me, I can make a lot of money for you, but you must do what I say." He continued: "The demon school-teacher has a horse that has never been beaten in a race. I am going to become a horse. You wager with him. He will put up two thousand dollars. He will want to buy me. He will offer you five thousand dollars for me. I shall beat his horse. Then sell me, but do not sell the bridle. I shall be 'blowed up' if you do."

So the old man went to see the devil about the race. They came to an agreement, and when the day set for it came, the boy turned into the most beautiful horse that had ever been seen; then he went to the starting point of the race. The race started and he won by more than a hundred feet. After the race the devil-school-teacher said to the old man: "You must sell me your horse."

The teacher knew that the winning horse was in reality the little boy who had assumed the shape of a beautiful horse. He said: "I will give you five thousand dollars for your horse if you will just let me have it." The old man was so poverty-stricken, he thought awhile and then said: "I will sell you the horse, but not the bridle." The old teacher then said: "I will give you five thousand dollars for the bridle." "Well," answered the old man, "take it."

The old man now had ten thousand dollars. The old teacher

took the horse to his servant and warned him never to remove the horse's bridle, but did not explain why. The little boy, now a horse, would not drink. They would lead him to the water's edge, but he just refused to drink. It was the same thing about food, he would not eat. One day, the servant said: "I am going to take that horse to the river and remove his bridle to see if he will drink. He is going to die anyway."

When the bridle was removed, the horse turned into a fish (patassa). He jumped into the river. The teacher turned into a larger fish (gar fish), and leaped after him. The little boy came out of the water and turned into a beautiful ring and dropped in front of a young lady, who was rocking in a rocking chair on the "gallery." The old devil turned into a hawk and kept going beyond the place where the ring was. Then he returned.

The young lady was sick, very sick. She was worried. The teacher advertised himself as a doctor who could cure any human ailment. The young lady's father saw the advertisement and he went to see the doctor. The doctor told him he would take the case under one condition: if he gave him the ring in payment and it must not be handed to him, but thrown on the floor. So he started treating the young lady, and when she was well, he said: "I shall come for my pay tomorrow."

The next day he returned. He sat down and said: "Throw it on the floor." It turned into a grain of corn and the devil turned into a rooster, the little boy turned into a wild cat (pichou) and ate the devil. That is why there is no devil today.

9

THE MILLIONAIRE, HIS DAUGHTER AND HER SUITORS

THERE WAS A MILLIONAIRE who had a very beautiful daughter. She was superior to other young ladies. He would say: "He who builds me a boat that will travel on land and water will get the hand of my daughter in marriage." Then there was an old woman who had three sons. She was very poor. The eldest son said to her: "Mother, will you cook a small. bread and a capon for me? I am going to see if I can build the millionaire's boat."

So she did, and he went. He arrived at a place where there was a small bayou with clear water. He said: "This is where I am going to eat my lunch." A stoop-shouldered old woman came to him. She asked: "Where are you going, my son?" He replied: "Old beggar, I am going to make paddles." "Well," she exclaimed, "paddles you will make." He kept on his way. At each stroke of the ax, a paddle would fly. This went on all day. At night he returned home and said nothing about his experience to his mother and brothers.

The second son asked his mother to cook a bread and a chicken for him. He would try his luck at building the boat. He went, and when he arrived at the bayou, the old woman appeared. She asked: "Where are you going, my son?" "Oh," he answered, "old curiosity box, it's none of your business. I am going to make bats." "Well," she said, "bats you will make." He went, but at every stroke of the ax, a bat would fly. This continued all day and at night he returned home.

The youngest one said to his mother the next day: "Prepare a lunch for me, bread and chicken. I want to see if I can build the boat." So he went to the bayou. The old woman appeared while he was unwrapping his lunch. He said to her: "Grandma, come and eat with me. I do not have much, but I should be very happy to divide what I have with you." She asked: "Where are you going?" He answered: "The millionaire promised his daughter in marriage and all the money he wanted to the one who could build a boat that would travel on land and water, so I am going to try." "Well," she cried, "I am going to eat with you and boats you will build right away."

So he left. He arrived early in the morning. At the first stroke of the ax, the tree fell, the second stroke, the hull was built. At the third stroke, the boat was almost finished. He took the machine and he started on his way to the millionaire of the town. He went a piece and came to a man who was running, then resting awhile. He had two large grindstones tied to his legs. The young man stopped his boat and asked him what in the world he was doing. "Well," he answered, "I am a good enough runner to beat the rabbits running with this handicap." "Well," the young man said, "get on my boat. I may need you." They kept on and came to a man who had his ear to the ground. The young man asked him what he was doing. He replied that he had planted a grain of wheat and he was listening to hear if it was coming up. "Well," the young man commanded, "get on my boat and let's go." When they had almost reached their destination, they saw a man licking a pork barrel. The young man told him to get on the boat.

When they arrived at the millionaire's home, the young man was told that before he could get the daughter and the money, he would have to get a man that could outrun her, carrying a pail of water, getting it at the spring a mile from where they stood. The young man was ready, having his rabbit chaser with him, who was willing to try this race. So they left. The rabbit chaser was so far ahead of the girl that he had to wait for her at the spring. She arrived and began looking for lice in his hair to try to put him to sleep, to delay him. The young man said to his good listener: "Will you listen to find out what they are doing?" He listened and said: "She is looking for lice in his hair to put him to sleep so she can win the race."

The young man said: "Shoot and hit the tip of his nose." The rabbit chaser won the race very easily. He then asked his pork eater if he could eat more pork than the girl. A large quantity of pork was prepared for the contest. The man won this race too. So the young man married the millionaire's daughter and gave the millionaire his boat.

10

THE MAN AND HIS THREE SONS

ONCE UPON A TIME a man had three sons, and as they reached twenty-one years of age, he would call them to him and tell them they had to go out into the world. He asked the eldest which he preferred, a thousand dollars or a thousand friends. "Oh," the young man answered, "a thousand dollars." The second son had the same answer, but the third one said he preferred a thousand friends. The father said to him: "Wherever you go, you will find friends, but your brothers will have to steal and plunder wherever they go."

So they left home and walked and walked. Wherever the youngest one went, he was well received. He was given presents, teas, he was asked to spend the day and the night, while the others paid wherever they went, arriving "broke" in a city. The youngest one came across a corpse on a sand reef. "Oh," he said, "you were too good a friend. I must make a grave for you. I shall make a wooden spade to dig a grave for you." He made the spade and buried the body. Then he went on his way. Soon the man appeared alive in front of him and said: "You were the only man to do anything for me. I shall give you the best present that ever anyone received. Here is a purse that will never be empty. You will always have a dollar left, no matter how much you spend. And here is a horn. You can call anyone to you that you wish. Then here is a belt. You put it on and it will take you to any place you wish to go."

So the young man was now a millionaire. He went to meet his brothers in the city, who were now very poor. He said to them: "Don't worry. I have enough money for all of us." So they began buying right and left, plots of land, etc. The eldest one fell in love with the king's daughter and one day he asked his brother for the purse. He said: "I am going to see her now and I want to have it in case of an emergency." When he arrived at the lady's house, she wanted to know how he happened to have so much money when just a short time before he was very poor. "You now own property in town, building lots, etc."

He answered: "It is a secret." "Well," she replied, "you must tell me, or I will not marry you." So he told her it was the purse he was holding, which was never empty. She grabbed it and ran into her bedroom. He had to go home and tell his brother that he had lost his purse. The brother said to him: "Take this belt to find where she is and take the purse away from her." When he appeared in the room, the young lady wanted to know how he had made his way in. No one had ever been able to do it before. He explained: "It's a secret." "Well, if you do not tell me, I will not marry you," she repeated. So he told her it was by the power of the belt. Just putting it on could transport one to any place one desired. She got it, put it on and immediately was moved to another room, leaving him alone. He struggled so hard that he succeeded in forcing his way out of the house and went straight to his brother to tell him the news. The brother said to him: "We have one article left, the horn. Take it and call a large enough army to fight the king's guard. He will send someone to ask for terms." So the brother went and called an army, but failed in the same manner as before. The brother was now ruined. He went home to tell his father the story.

One day he was sitting at a street corner, bemoaning his fate, when his dead friend appeared again. He said to him: "You are ruined, but it is not your fault, it is your brother's fault. I will help you again. Here are some beautiful figs. They can make one's nose enlarge. Sell them to the young lady only. And here is a powder which can reduce the size of one's nose when used. Pose as a doctor who can cure any kind of inflammation and go see the girl."

The brother did so. He went to the king's palace. The trick worked. He asked the purse, the belt and the horn in payment for the cure. He began treating the girl's nose and it began getting smaller and smaller. As soon as it was normal, she delivered the articles and he returned to his brothers.

11

THE MILLER

ONCE UPON A TIME there was a man who was very, very poor. He was a widower with an only daughter. The king lost his wife just as the little daughter reached maturity. The old miller was so very poor—all in the world he had was his mill to grind corn—that he told his daughter: "I must try to get the king to marry you so as not to be so poor."

So he went to the king's house. He said to him: "I have a daughter who is just perfect. She can do anything she wants to do; she can turn hay into gold." "Well," the king replied, "bring her here. I shall give her a roomful of hay to turn into gold. If she can turn hay into gold, I am going to marry her, for she will be perfect."

So the poor man went very early with his daughter to the palace. After taking a seat in the room, she began to weep because she felt that she could not do it. A little old fellow arrived. He was about three feet high. His big toes were eight inches long and his fingers and thumbs were ten inches long. He asked the girl: "What is the matter with you, miller's daughter?" She answered: "I shall be destroyed tonight. I would have to spin all this hay into gold. I cannot." Then he asked: "What will you give me if I do it for you? Will you give me the ring you are wearing on your finger?" "Oh, yes," she replied.

So the little fellow began working with his long feet, thumbs and fingers, and in a short time all the hay had become gold threads rolled as a ball. The king came and took the young lady home. He said to her: "In order to be very sure, tomorrow I shall take you to a room twice as large. If you can convert the hay into gold, I shall marry you; if not, you will be destroyed."

Again, the poor girl wept. The same little fellow came to her. He wanted to know why she was crying and she told him the story. He said: "Don't cry. What will you give me to spin your hay?" She answered: "I have nothing." "Well," he replied, "give me the kerchief around your neck." "Of course you can have it," she exclaimed. That night the king returned. The task was done. He said he wanted to be very certain of her ability so he would place her in a room twice as large. If she could spin it all, she would have everything she wanted and he would marry her.

So back she went into a very large room filled with hay. She began crying. The same little fellow appeared and said to her: "What will you give me to spin the hay into threads of gold today?" "Well," she answered, "I have absolutely nothing left. Nothing." He asked: "Will you give me the first child you will have after you are queen?" She was so worried that she agreed. So he spun the room full of hay and he left.

Two years after she married, she had a very beautiful baby. When it was three days old, the little fellow came to her bed. He said: "I came to get what you promised me." She had a fainting spell, she was so perturbed over losing her child. The little fellow was sorry for her. He said: "I will give you three days to find out what my name is. If you can learn what my name is, I shall leave you your child; if not, I shall take it."

The next day she sent people everywhere to take down the names they heard. The next morning the little fellow returned. He asked: "Well, what's my name this morning?" She began telling all kinds of names. Every time she pronounced a name, he would say: "That's not it! That's not it!"

The second day she sent people much farther into the kingdom to take down all the names they heard. The next morning the little fellow returned and said: "I came to find out what my name is, if you have learned my name." She had a long list of names which she pronounced for him, but to each name he would say: "That's not my name." He repeated: "You have until tomorrow. If you do not know my name tomorrow, I shall take the child."

So during the night she sent people in every direction, into strange places, to take down names. There was a man going across a dense woods. He saw a big fire afar, and a small man with large feet and long fingers, who was jumping up and down in the fire and he was saying: "Today I burn, tomorrow I shall bloom. What luck! The queen's child will come take my place. No one knows what my name is. My name is *Rompetailtailskin.*"

So the man listened and took the name down. He went back to the king's wife and told her: "I have the name." He related to her how he had seen the little old man, what he had done, and how he had pronounced his name.

The next morning, the little fellow returned and wanted to know for the last time what his name was. She answered: "Your name is Joe." He replied: "No." "Your name is George." "No." "Your name is Lee." "No." Then she said: "Perhaps your name is *Rompetailtailskin.*" He remarked: "The devil told you." At this moment, the floor caved in all around his feet. He disappeared under the house and that was the end of him.

12

MOUSTAPHAT

ONCE UPON A TIME there was a woman who had a son. She could not make him work. At seventeen he still would not do a thing. She tried for a whole year to make him help her, but he would not. So she told him he had to leave home if he would not help her to make a living. He went to spend the night at his godmother's home. She was a sorceress. He told her his story. "Well," she said, "I shall give you a magic wand. You will strike it against something and say 'by the virtue of my little

wand, may I have such and such a thing,' anything you may
wish. It will make you a living."

The young man thanked her and went on his way. He got
a job. He sewed a big sack and got into it. When his boss went
to see him, he found him in the sack. He was too lazy to move.
The boss ripped the sack open and began kicking him; he chased
him away. He left and passed by the princess' house. She was
very beautiful. She was on the porch. He said: "By the virtue
of my wand, may the princess have a child and may it have a
ball of gold in its hand at birth and may the king have everyone
pass by the child and may the child hand me the ball of gold."

Years rolled by and Moustafat kept on traveling. He had
everything he wanted with the magic wand. The child was born
and the king had all his subjects pass by the child. Many of
them were millionaires. Moustafat went. He hid behind the door.
The king saw him and said: "Get out." When Moustafat passed
by the bed, the child handed him the ball of gold. It angered
the king. He had him put on a boat with his daughter.

He related to her how his godmother had given him a magic
wand and he could get anything he wanted. She asked him to
get a small spoon to feed her child who was crying. Moustafat
did so. Then she asked him to wish that he was as bright as he
was stupid. He did so. Then she wanted him to wish he were
as handsome as he was homely, that he look as nice as any
man in her father's kingdom. He did so. He was then the best-
looking, the brightest young man that had ever been known.

Then she said: "Now wish that we may find ourselves in a
beautiful house built tonight opposite Father's house, the place
where he sent us adrift on the water, also a bridge, so that he
may be able to visit us and see what we have." He made the
wish and they found themselves at daybreak in a house much
more beautiful than the king's. There was a beautiful bridge
across the river. When the king arose, he went straight to the
bridge. He began looking at the building. He said to his daughter, whom he had not recognized: "How does it happen that
your building is much more beautiful than mine? I thought I
had the most beautiful house in town."

13

POUCETTE
(Tom Thumb)

ONCE UPON A TIME there was a married couple who had eight
children. They were poor. One night they decided to go lose
them in the woods. But Poucette, who was no larger than one's
thumb, had hidden under a chair and had heard all the plans.

He filled his pockets with pebbles. The father left with the
intention of losing them, but Poucette dropped pebbles all the
way as they walked. After the father left them in the forest, he
returned home and Poucette returned also with the children.
The father and mother pretended they were happy to see them;
they gave them something to eat.

That night the parents planned to try again, but Poucette
heard them. He filled his pockets with flour this time, and the
next day, dropped flour all the way into the woods. The father
returned home and later Poucette thought he would do the
same, but the birds had eaten the flour and he could not find
the way.

They walked and walked until they came to a small house
where a giant lived. He was not at home, but his wife was there.
She said to them: "When my husband returns, he will eat you
up." Poucette asked to hide. She gave them something to eat
and hid them under a large box.

The giant came home and said: "My, it smells fresh meat."
She replied: "Yes, but promise that you will not kill them and
I shall tell you." He promised he would not kill them. She put
the children in a separate bed and they stayed in bed. She
happened to have eight children, too, and put on hers, blue
caps, and on the others, white ones. During the night, Poucette
got up and exchanged the caps.

The giant went to the beds to kill the visitors. He looked at the caps and thought those wearing white caps were the strangers, so he killed all eight of them. Before daylight, Poucette and his brothers and sisters got up and left and this time they found their way home.

14

ROCLORE

NUMBER ONE

ONCE UPON A TIME there was a man whose name was Roclore. He lived quite near the king's house. The king had bought what is called a blower, or bellows, for his wife to light the fire every morning, and Roclore wanted one very much for his wife.

One morning he got up and said to his wife: "If you wish to come with me, you may. I am going to win the beautiful bellows which the king has." So she got ready and went with him. Roclore said to the king: "Sir, I came to ask your permission to do something. Allow me to give a *soufflet* to my wife this morning." (*Soufflet* means a pair of bellows, but also a slap in the face.) The king replied: "Roclore, you may do so, but not too hard."

Roclore got up and stood on the tip of his shoes. He went and reached for the bellows. He handed it to his wife and said: "Here it is." The king exclaimed: "Roclore, I forbid you to set foot on my land." What did Roclore do? He went home. He hitched his horse to the buggy, filled the front of it with his own soil. Then he passed by the king's house, tapping his foot and whistling as loudly as he could. The king uttered these words: "Roclore, didn't I tell you not to set foot on my soil?"

Roclore shouted: "My feet are on my soil, sir. They are not at all on your soil. Well, sir, if you wish, I'll wager you that I can steal tonight your horse which is in the stable." The king answered: "Of course you cannot." They settled on one hundred dollars. What did the king do? He hired four men, one to hold the horse's bridle, one for each stirrup, and one for the tail. He told them that Roclore was coming to steal the horse. They must be sure not to go to sleep. They had wagered one hundred dollars.

What did Roclore do during the night? He dressed like an old woman. He went in front of the stable where the men were watching the king's horse. He said to the men: "I am traveling tonight and I do not have a place to lay my head on. If you will take me in for the night, I shall give you drinks. I have some very good whiskey."

They were very willing and invited him in right away, calling him "old woman," for that was his disguise. He began serving them drinks, got them so intoxicated that they dropped to the ground, but kept on holding to the bridle, etc. Roclore cut the straps of the stirrups, they fell to the ground; then he cut the reins of the bridle and it fell; then he cut the end of the tail and it fell to the ground. He took the horse out very quietly and left.

At dawn he arrived at the king's home on the king's horse, which was trotting at a fast gait. Roclore exclaimed: "Hello, sir, here's your horse." The king said: "Roclore, you are terrible!" "Well, that's nothing," added Roclore, "I can steal the sheet off your bed tonight." "That you cannot do," replied the king. "Well," said Roclore, "let's wager." They settled on the amount.

When night came, the king placed a man at each window and one at each door while he sat at the foot of his bed. A little while later, Roclore brought his stuffed man out. The king shot at it. Roclore let it fall by means of sticks he manipulated. Everybody rushed out, thinking Roclore had been killed. Roclore, in the confusion, went inside the dark at the queen's bed and said: "Give me the sheet. I have killed him." She rolled up the sheet and handed it to him, thinking it was her husband's request.

A little later they came into the house, saying the "stuffed man" and not Roclore had been shot. "Oh," the king exclaimed, "Roclore has my sheet. He came and got it." So Roclore called at the king's home the next morning, saying: "Here's your sheet. I came to return it to you."

"Well," said the king, "Roclore, I can stand this no longer. I am going to drown you to finish with you once for all." He stuck him in a large sack and then went in front of a saloon. He went in and left Roclore at the gate. He took many drinks. A shepherd driving sheep came by. Roclore began screaming: "I don't want, I don't want." The shepherd said: "What is it you don't want?" Roclore answered in the sack: "The king wants me to marry his daughter, but I don't want to marry her. I am going to drown him."

"Well," said the shepherd, "I am willing. Put me in the sack. I am willing to marry the king's daughter." "Well," cried Roclore, "untie the sack and I shall put you in it." The shepherd untied the sack. Roclore put him in it and he got on the horse, driving the sheep in front of him.

The next day he passed by the king's home crying: "Sheep, sheep, sheep." The king said: "He is calling me." "Oh, sir, do you wish to buy fat sheep?" Said the king: "Did I not drown you yesterday?" "Sir, if you had thrown me a little further, I would have come out with a fine herd of cattle." "Well, if that's it, you must throw me into the water." So Roclore stuck him in the sack and pitched him in the river, but that one never returned.

15

ROCLORE
NUMBER TWO

THE KING HAD A SERVANT whose name was Roclore. The king was angry with this servant. For that reason, he cut Roclore's horses' tails. Then Roclore split the king's horses' mouths. The king then told his servant not to say that his horses had died. Roclore said that the horses could neither eat nor drink. The king said: "They are dead then." "No," said Roclore, "I did not say that." The king was tired of Roclore and told him to leave. He just did not want him to pass by his house any more, so the servant left, but returned the next day. The king wanted to know why, after he had been told to keep away. Roclore answered that he was not going by but simply crossing the road. The king ordered him never to set his foot on the king's land. Roclore got soil somewhere else, put it in his buggy and returned.

The king asked him why he had returned when he had been forbidden to set his foot on the king's property. Roclore answered that he was on soil from the neighboring parish and not on the king's soil.

The king told him he was just too smart. Roclore offered to wager him that he could remove the sheet off his bed at nine o'clock that night. The king accepted. Roclore made a "stuffed monkey" with old clothes, the likeness of a man. He tied a cord to it in order to pull it when desired. He put a pulley at the top of the window. The king was seated at the window holding his gun. He fired when he saw the clown through the window. He thought he had killed Roclore, but while he went out to see, Roclore went around the house and went in through a window. He got the sheet and won the wager.

The king tried to drown Roclore. He was carrying his servant in a sack to the river bank. But the king got thirsty and went in a house for water. At that time, the shepherd passed by with his sheep. He asked what was in the sack. Roclore answered that he was the king's servant. The shepherd wanted to know why he was in a sack. Roclore replied that the king wanted him to marry his daughter. "Well," said the shepherd, "I am willing to marry the king's daughter." Roclore told him to unfasten the sack and he would exchange places with him. Roclore tied the sack after putting the shepherd in it, then drove the sheep to their destination. The king came out, picked up the sack, went to the river and threw it in, drowning the shepherd.

The next day, Roclore again went by the king's home, this time with his sheep. The king recognized him and wanted to know where the sheep came from. "Oh," said Roclore, "you did not throw me far enough into the river. I could see more sheep deeper in the water." The king said: "Come, throw me into the river." Roclore put him in a sack and threw him into the river. And that was the end of the king. Roclore then became king.

16

THE LITTLE BIRD
O R
THE SINGING BONES

ONCE UPON A TIME a married couple had two children, a son and a daughter. One morning, the man left to go to work and the woman said to her two children: "Go get me some chips."

So they went. The little girl gathered chips, but the little boy pulled out his pocket knife and began digging little wells. The little sister said: "Pick up the chips to make fire to bake cakes. You will not have any cakes if you do not gather chips."

When they went into the house, the little girl said: "Mother, my little brother just would not gather chips." "Well," replied the mother, "he will not have any cakes next time. Go get your cookies in the barrel." When the little boy leaned over the side of the barrel to reach for the cookies, she cut his head off with the large knife and she cooked him for dinner.

At noon when the father returned for dinner, all the way home a little bird would follow him and sing:

> "My mother killed me,
> My father will eat me,
> My little sister will gather
> My bones in her tiny sacred
> Handkerchief."

When the father arrived at the gate, the little bird repeated:

> "My mother killed me,
> My father will eat me,
> My little sister will gather
> My bones in her tiny handkerchief."

The man entered. Immediately he smelled fresh meat cooking and asked: "Where did you get fresh meat?" The wife replied: "The neighbors sent me fresh meat. I am preparing a good dinner."

The little girl said: "I do not want to eat. I shall get under the table and gather my little brother's bones." "Well," asked her father, "what does she mean with that story?" The mother added: "She is just talking to be talking. You must not let that bother you."

While they were eating, the same little bird came back, lighted on the gate post and sang the same song. The mother said to the little girl: "Go chase that bird away." She did, and returned wearing a beautiful dress. "Well," said the father, "next time I shall go." A little while later, the bird returned and sang the same song:

> "My mother killed me,
> My father will eat me,
> My little sister will gather
> My bones in her tiny handkerchief."

The father went and returned wearing nice new clothes. The mother said: "When the bird returns, I shall go chase it away." The bird returned and sang the same song:

> "My mother killed me,
> My father will eat me,
> My little sister will gather
> My bones in her tiny handkerchief."

The mother went out, but when she arrived at the steps lightning struck her and turned her into dust. Since then, there is dust.

17

LITTLE JOHN
('Tit Jean)
NUMBER ONE

THE PRINCESS HAD PROMISED to marry the man who could run faster than she. Little John said he would try to outrun her. On the way, he met a man who was lying down. Little John asked him what he was doing there. He replied that he had planted a pea there seven years before. He was listening to the pea's coming up. Little John told him he was the man he needed. The good listener joined Little John.

Farther on he met another man. This man had a bow and arrow. Little John asked him whom he wanted to kill with this arrow. He replied that he wanted to kill a swallow at the tip end of a cloud. He was going to cut off the bird's beak. Little John hired the good marksman too.

A little later he met a third man. This one was sitting down in the middle of the prairie. Little John asked him what he was doing there. The man pointed to three windmills near by. It was his work to blow hard enough to make them function. Little John hired the good blower.

Further on, Little John met another man. He had wheels of cork tied to his legs. Little John asked him why in the world he wore the cork. The man explained that it was a device to keep from running too fast when he was running after deer and rabbits. Little John hired him, saying he was the very man he needed.

The men reached the place where they were to run. They had to get a bottle at the well and return with it. He who did first, would win the race. Little John gave the bottle to Good Runner and he went to the other end to see the race. The race started between the princess and Good Runner. She saw that he was getting ahead, so she asked him to stop and rest with her. They sat down on the ground. She looked at his head. He was resting it on an old skull. Good Runner went to sleep. She picked up the bottle and started running.

Little John asked Good Listener to listen to find out if they were coming. He answered only one was coming. His runner was sleeping on an ox head. Little John told Good Marksman to fire at Good Runner. He did, and cut the ox head with his arrow so as to remove it. Good Runner picked up his bottle and started running in an effort to catch up with the princess who was ahead. Little John wished his Good Listener to listen again. He reported that the princess was still far ahead.

Little John told Good Blower to blow in order to stop the princess who was coming too fast. He blew and stopped her and he won the race as well as the princess for Little John.

18

LITTLE JOHN
('Tit Jean)
NUMBER TWO

ONCE UPON A TIME there was a man who had an only son. His name was Little John. He went to school until he was graduated. Then his father asked his son: "What profession or business are you interested in?" "Well," he replied, "Papa, it is hunting." "Hunting!" exclaimed the father. "Yes," replied the son. "Well, we can go with you tomorrow," said the father. So they got ready. He said: "We shall go to the home of an old man by the name of Simon." The boy answered: "All right."

They went, and the old man told the boy it would take him a year and a half to learn to hunt. When he had been there a year, it was said that a deer would get in the king's garden. As a prize to the young man who killed the animal, the king would give him his daughter in marriage. Little John asked his master if he thought that he was a good enough hunter to enter the contest. Simon assured him that he could. So they planned to leave the next day to go see the king.

He went, and arrived in the afternoon. After much discussion with the king, they came to an agreement. He was to have three trials at shooting the said deer. The king agreed to giving him his daughter in marriage for getting rid of the deer, which, he said, got in the garden to eat every morning at six.

The next morning, Little John got up before daylight, got ready and went into the garden. At six the deer jumped over the fence and was in the garden. Little John fired his rifle and missed. The deer got away. The young man began to worry, for he was to be killed if he did not succeed with three trials.

So he made plans to try the next day. He got up even earlier. He went into the garden and fired when the deer returned. Again, he missed. And now he was really worried. He went to the king and asked him if he could get a substitute for the last trial. The king gave him permission to do so.

Little John telephoned his old teacher and asked him to come. Simon replied that he could be there that night. He left riding a small, skinny, white mare. He saw a large horse tied in a field. Simon had the habit of talking to himself. He said: "Simon, get down and exchange horses, your little mare for the big horse. No, do not take that horse. He is not yours." He went farther and saw a small, pretty, black mare. He said to himself: "Well, you are going to trade horses." He got off his horse, removed the saddle and tied his horse in the place of the little black mare that he led out of the field. As he was saddling the mare, she said to him: "Put the saddle on tight, for I travel very, very fast. Faster than the wind. And be sure never to forget me."

She continued: "Tomorrow when you are going to saddle me before daylight, we will go into the garden, but you will not kill the deer. He is going to try to swim across the river.

While he is in the water, shoot, and you will kill him. On our way back, we shall go through a beautiful town. There will be many interesting things to look at, but you must not touch a thing." "All right," replied Simon.

He arrived at the king's late in the afternoon. His intention was to kill the deer the next morning. Preparation for the wedding of Little John and the princess was in progress. "Tomorrow we shall go hunting," he said.

So he got up early the next morning, he fed his little mare, he got ready, he saddled the horse before six, and then he went into the garden. After a while, at six, the deer jumped over the fence and into the garden. Simon got his horse and followed the deer, which now jumped out of the garden, and Simon after him on his horse. This went on for five or six miles and there the deer leaped into the river. Then Simon fired and killed the deer. Then he said: "What am I going to do?" The horse answered: "That's nothing. We shall go get it on the other side of the river." He wanted the tongue only. So he went and got it. Then he set out for the king's home. They went slowly. They passed through a large town where they saw many things, large dolls on the side of the street. He said to himself: "Simon, take that doll. No, do not take it."

They set out again. A little later they came to a more beautiful town and pretty dolls. "Well," he said to himself, "Simon, you will have to take that doll. Good." So he had it wrapped in a paper and he put it in his pocket and he left. Late that afternoon they arrived at the king's home. The king said: "Tomorrow we shall get ready for the wedding of my daughter and Little John."

After while old Simon began to nod; he was tired and sleepy. He leaned to one side and the king saw the doll in his pocket. He asked: "Simon, what do you have in your pocket?" "Oh," he replied, "nothing." "Oh, yes, I want to see it," said the king. Simon had to show it to him. Then the king told him that he, Simon, had to get him the lady in whose likeness the doll had been made or he would kill him.

So Simon went to the stable where his little mare was. She

said to him: "Simon, that's nothing. Saddle me, and we shall go to the lady's home." He saddled her and they went to the village and he found the young woman in whose likeness the doll had been made. He asked her father if he wanted to buy a horse. "Oh, yes," replied the father, "that's exactly what I want for my daughter." "Well, I have one to sell," replied Simon. "There's this one. Let your daughter ride behind me to try her and I shall sell her to you." "All right," responded the father.

So the young woman got on behind Simon. He rode on to the king's home as fast as the wind. He said to the king: "Here she is." The king was a widower. "Well, we shall have a double wedding," said the king. So Simon went to the barn to put his mare in the stable. She said to him: "You must never forget me." Simon replied: "Oh, no! I would never do that. You have saved my life."

The wedding party was gay, there were many cakes, the bridegroom was on the "go" all the time. Simon forgot his little mare. He thought of her the next morning and went to the stable. She had fallen to the ground and was dying. He got very much worried. He exclaimed: "What am I to do to save your life?" She replied: "Cut my head off. That will save my life."

"Well," he answered, "you have always told me what to do and I succeeded." So he took his dagger and cut the horse's head off. To his surprise, there crawled out of that skin a young lady of twenty-five. He took her by the arm [hooked arms] and went in the back yard where there were large pots of boiling grease and cracklings. He said: "If I knew that by diving in that hot grease I would come out looking twenty-five years of age, I would dive." So he dived and he came out at the other end, looking twenty-five. He accompanied his young lady up the stairs.

The king was surprised and wanted to know how he had rejuvenated. He asked the king to accompany him; he would show him. He told the king to dive in that hot grease and he would come out on the other side looking twenty-five years of age. The king did as he was told, but he came out a crackling—fried. That was the end of him. That is why there is no king today.

19

LITTLE JOHN
('Tit Jean)
NUMBER THREE

LITTLE JOHN HAD PLAYED cards with the devil and had lost a year's time. So the devil told him to come the next day, early in the morning, and he would tell him what to do for a whole year. The next morning, Little John called at the door: "It is I, Little John, come to begin work." "Well," replied the devil, "here's a wooden ax. I have a forest. I wish you to convert it into a desert."

Little John picked up the ax and went to the scene for work. He sat down and began to weep. At twelve the devil sent his youngest daughter, Blancaflor, with his lunch. She found him crying. She asked him why. He explained that he had lost a year's time gambling with her father and now he was told to fell all the trees in the forest with a wooden ax. He simply could not do it. She said: "Be courageous; eat your lunch, then lie across my knees."

He did as he was told. She had a magic wand which she waved, saying: "By the virtue of my little wand, may this forest be changed to a desert according to my father's wish." At that very moment, everything changed as the devil desired.

She said to Little John: "Now, tomorrow morning you will come to deliver your day's work and get your assignment for tomorrow. He will invite you to enter, but do not enter. Tell him you have come for your assignment."

So the next morning, Little John knocked at the devil's door. The devil said: "Who is there?" Little John replied: "It is I, Little John, your hired man. I came to deliver my day's work and get · my next assignment." The devil remarked: "You are very. early. Come in and have a cup of coffee." "No, thank you," said Little John. "I must get my work and return home." The devil told him that his task was to empty the feather bed in the desert, scatter the feathers, then gather them and put them back where they were and return the bed without losing a single feather the next night.

Little John left. When he arrived in the desert, he emptied the feather bed and scattered the feathers. He sat down on the ground and wept bitterly. At that moment, Blancaflor arrived with his lunch. She asked him why he was crying. "Well, you saved me once, but you cannot this time. I am lost." She repeated her advice to eat his lunch and to lie across her knees. Then she used her magic wand to gather all the feathers, without losing a single one, according to the desire of her father. It was done.

Blancaflor said to him: "Little John, you will go even earlier tomorrow and knock at my father's door. He will ask: 'Who is there?' Answer, 'Your hired man, who came to bring his work and get his next assignment.'"

Little John did exactly as Blancaflor had advised him. The devil invited him in, but he declined, saying: "I want my next assignment, so I can go home." The devil's task was that Little John was to exchange the position of two arms of the sea. Little John made his way to the sea, sat down and began to cry. Blancaflor came with his lunch and found him crying. She said: "That's nothing. Eat your lunch and then lie across my knees." Little John replied: "Blancaflor, you saved my life twice, but this time you cannot. I am lost."

He lay down as directed and she said: "By the virtue of my wand, may the arms of the sea exchange positions according to my father's desire." It was done immediately. Blancaflor warned

Little John to come earlier the next day and not to enter the house.

Little John knocked at the devil's home very early the next morning. He was invited to enter for a cup of coffee but he declined again, giving as an excuse the wish to start his task right away. The devil assigned: "I lost a clarinet seven years ago. If you can find it and return it as it was when new, it will end your work and you may have any one of my three daughters in marriage—your choice."

So Little John left. He went to the sea, sat down and began to weep as before. After while, Blancaflor came and said: "You are again crying." He replied: "Blancaflor, you saved my life three times, but this time, it is impossible. I am lost." She repeated: "That's nothing. Eat your lunch, then lie across my knees." Then she uttered the magic words: "By the virtue of my wand, may my father's clarinet be found and brought to him as he desires." She then explained to him that he would have to cut her up in pieces and throw them into the sea and gather her blood in a gourd. Then call each piece from the sea, one at a time, and put them in place, using her blood to make them stick—not to forget any piece. "Oh," he exclaimed, "I can never do this to you when you have been so kind to me." She said: "You will have to do it." So he began the task of cutting up her body and throwing the pieces into the sea. When he was through, he called one piece at a time and put it in place. The last piece was the hand. It came holding the clarinet. He had forgotten a finger. Blancaflor said to him: "Little John, you have forgotten a finger. Father has promised you a daughter in marriage. He will have us place a hand in a crack in the wall. I am going to use the hand with a finger missing."

The next morning, Little John knocked at the devil's door. The devil said: "Who is there?" Little John replied: "It is I, Little John, your hired man, who comes with your clarinet." The devil said: "Come in, Little John. I promised you a daughter in marriage. You will choose. I shall have them put a hand through a crack in the wall. The one you will touch will be yours." Little John touched the one with a missing finger,

Blancaflor's. The devil said: "Little John, you made a wise choice. I promised to let you choose, I am going to keep my promise."

So they were married. Blancaflor told Little John that they would have to leave that night because her father would eat them the next day, if they remained at home. "He has a pair of boots that cover three leagues in one step and a mule that covers the distance of seven leagues in one step. You wear the boots, and we shall both ride the mule."

She took three peas and placed them in a glass. She took a piece of soap, a comb, and a piece of sponge. She put the glass with the peas on the table and then left.

The next morning the devil called: "Blancaflor." The pea answered: "Little Father." "Get up." "Yes, Father." After while he called again: "Blancaflor, get up." The second pea answered: "Yes, Father, I am getting up." But the devil did not hear a sound. He repeated: "Blancaflor." The third pea answered: "Little Father." "My, but you are lazy since you are married." "Yes, Father, I am getting up."

All this time Little John and Blancaflor were walking and walking. After while they saw a big black cloud. She said to him: "Look, this black cloud is Papa." They became two ducks in a pond, but the devil was coming too fast. She said to Little John: "Drop the piece of soap." He did, while they kept walking on and on. The devil was getting close, so she told Little John to drop the comb. It formed a mountain of combs and the devil cut himself on them. They kept on walking. The devil was about to catch up with them when she told Little John to drop the sponge. The devil sank on the sponge. Blancaflor and Little John reached the home of his parents safely.

Blancaflor said to Little John: "Go in and get me some clothes. I am not clean enough to go in at your parents' home. Do not let your parents kiss you, because you will then forget me." Little John went in and asked for clothes for his wife and told them not to kiss him. His mother began looking for clothes for him to bring his wife. While she was busy, a little sister came in from playing in the yard and, catching him around the neck from the rear, kissed him.

His mother reminded him: "Little John, your clothes are ready." He answered: "I have never asked you for any clothes." He remained with his parents and Blancaflor took refuge with neighbors.

Some time later, Little John began making plans to remarry. On the wedding day, Blancaflor bought two dolls, a little man that she called Little John, and a little woman, Blancaflor. Then she asked the owner of the house to give her permission to have the two dolls talk.

The doll Blancaflor said to the doll Little John: "Do you remember when you gambled with the devil and lost a year's time? He gave you the task of turning a forest into a desert and I helped you with my magic wand? Do you remember, Little John?" The doll Little John answered: "Yes, I remember." "*Craque.*" The wand hit the doll Little John. The man felt it too. "Do you remember, Little John, when I found you crying in despair because you could not pick up the feathers in the forest, and put them back in the feather bed? Do you remember when I helped you?" "Yes," answered the doll Little John. "*Craque*" on his head went the little wand. Little John himself felt the blow.

"Do you remember, Little John, when I found you in despair because you could not find my father's clarinet and I told you to cut my body up and throw the pieces into the sea and when you put them back together, you forgot one finger? Do you remember? See my hand?" The doll Little John said: "Yes, I remember." "*Craque*" went the wand on the head of the doll Little John. Little John scratched his head and said: "Yes, I remember." Then, Little John went to the owner of the house and said: "If you were to lose a key and bought a new one, and on your way back you should find the old one, which would you keep?" The man answered: "Oh! the old one." "Well," said Little John, "take back your daughter and I will take back my wife."

20

THE POOR MAN'S SON

ONCE UPON A TIME a man had a son. When the son became of age, he said: "Father, I must get a job." He went to see a very rich man. The man hired him but said he could not pay him until Christmas.

At Christmastime the rich man called him and said: "My good man, work for me another year and I shall pay you at the end of the year for two years' work." The young man answered: "All right." When Christmas rolled around again, the story was repeated. "Good man, will you work for me another year? I shall then pay you for three years' work," said the employer. At the end of the third year, he called the young man and paid him, saying: "My good workman, you have worked three years without ever complaining; we never quarreled. Here's a gun with which you can kill anything at any distance; here's a violin, anyone hearing it will dance without ever stopping; here's a hat, which will make you invisible whenever you put it on. You have completed your work. I do not need you any more."

So the young man left and walked until he came to another rich man who was interested in a small bird that flew high above the ground. A small red bird, a peculiar red. He said to the young man: "I would pay a big price for that bird." The young man answered: "I can shoot it." The bird fell in a pile of thick briars. The rich man had to go get it. While he was in the briars, the young man began to play his violin. The rich man began to dance, tearing his skin in the briars. He offered a thousand dollars to the young man to help him out of his predicament—to sell him the violin. The young man agreed.

The rich man reported the young man for a wretch. The case was tried and the young man was found guilty. The judge sentenced the man to hang. He read the sentence. He was charged with having made the man dance. When the judge called his deputies to take the prisoner to jail, he "tuned up" his violin and began to play. The judge, the lawyers, and everybody in the courthouse began to dance. They begged for peace. It amused the young man very much. At the end of the day, the judge offered to let him go "scot free" and to give him a thousand dollars if he stopped his music. He agreed, signed the agreement, and left.

III. COMICAL TALES

21

THE HUNCHBACK

Once there were three brothers who were poor. The youngest one was called Hunchback. He was employed by the king for fifty dollars until the cuckoo sang his first song. The condition was that both should be satisfied. The first one to complain would have a strip of skin two inches wide removed from his back.

Hunchback's first task was to cut wood without eating. The king's dog had eaten nis lunch and he could not complain. The second day, he cut the dog's head off and the king could not complain. The third day, the source of the trouble was the king's hogs. Hunchback had to tend them in the woods. Hunchback sold all of them for a thousand dollars, reserving the tails and the three leanest hogs. He stuck them and the tails in the mud; then he went to the king to tell him that all his hogs were stuck in the mud.

The fourth day, the king gave him cattle to tend. Again, he sold them all except the thinnest one which he hung in the top of a tree and told the king a cyclone had hung them all in the trees.

The king was in despair. He asked his mother-in-law for a way to get rid of Hunchback. She told him he would have to imitate the cuckoo, get up in a tree. She told him that she could climb the tree and do it.

When the king told Hunchback that the cuckoo had sung and the agreement was no longer valid, Hunchback answered that it was not the season for cuckoos to sing. It had to be killed. He got his gun and shot the mother-in-law. The king was unhappy and he said so. Hunchback cut a strip of skin off the king's back and also received fifty dollars and left.

22

FOOLISH JOHN

NUMBER ONE

FOOLISH JOHN WORRIED HIS MOTHER a great deal. She sent him to get a big pot. He went, and was returning with it when he arrived at a fork in the road. He said to the pot: "You see these two roads? Well, they both lead to our home." He placed the pot in one and he took the other saying: "You have three legs and I have two; let's see who will get home first."

When he reached home, his mother wanted to know where the pot was. He explained that the pot was to come home by a different road and that with three legs, it should have gotten home before him. She whipped him and sent him for the pot. It had disappeared. His mother told him they would have to pay for the neighbor's pot. It cost seven dollars. She gave him the money and he set out.

On the way he heard spring frogs singing in the pond. They sang: " '*Tite huit, 'tite huit, 'tite huit.*" ('*Tite* eight.) Foolish John said: "You are lying. I have seven." They continued their song: " '*Tite huit, 'tite huit, 'tite huit.*" He asked them to stop it, but they continued their tune. He threw his money into the pond and asked them to count it and see if he had eight.

He went back home and his mother wanted to know if he had returned the money. He replied that he had given it to the frogs. She whipped him again.

One day she sent him to borrow flour from the neighbor. When he was returning with the flour, he saw a hill of ants. He said to himself that the poor ants were hungry. So he gave them the flour. When he got home, his mother wanted to know where the flour was. He replied that the poor ants were so hungry he had given it to them. She whipped him.

Another time she sent him to get lard. On the way home, he saw cracks in the ground. He put all the lard in the cracks. When he got home, his mother asked him what he had done with the lard. He explained that the ground was so chapped he had greased it with the lard. She whipped him again.

His mother had a setting goose. Each time that Foolish John would pass by the goose, it would "sing" and try to peck him. He picked up a stick and killed it. He was sorry to see the eggs go to waste; he was afraid of his mother. He imagined to sit on the eggs himself. There were feathers in a box and tar in a barrel. He decided to use them in an effort to look more like a goose. He then played the part of a setting goose. His mother saw him, came with her whip and spanked him again. He ran to the small pond and swam like a goose. Foolish John was spanked again.

He ran away, but returned home after a few years. He told his mother he had learned of a remedy for their sick cow. It was necessary to lift her to the roof of the house and make her eat the moss or lichen growing there. This lichen was called polypod.

Foolish John built ladders and scaffolds to get the cow on the roof. His mother scolded him and told him that he was still Foolish John, he had not improved.

He went near the fireplace to get warm. It was too hot. He shouted to remove the chimney. His mother gave up.

FOOLISH JOHN

NUMBER TWO

THERE WAS ONCE UPON A TIME a small boy called Foolish John. One day his mother, before going to the field, said to him: "Son, you will churn the butter today and go to the market to sell it." "Yes, Mother."

As soon as his mother leaves, Foolish John starts the task of making the butter. When the butter is separated from the milk, he washes it, salts it and places it in a dish. He puts on his linen coat and his straw hat and leaves for the village with his butter. Since it had not rained for sometime, the ground was full of cracks.

"Poor road," said Foolish John, "how you must suffer with all those cracks! Wait a while, I am going to take care of you. When I am chapped, my mother rubs me with butter and it feels better."

He takes some of his butter and fills in the cracks with it. One can imagine how quickly his butter disappeared. "Wait," he says, "until I go home for some more. I am so sorry for you." He goes to the house and gets all the butter he can find and once more he spreads it all over the road. When he is finished, he returns home very well pleased with himself. When his mother returns, she asks him if he succeeded in churning the butter and if he sold it well.

"Don't speak to me about it! I churned it all right, but I did not have any to sell. I did not have enough to sell."

"Well, what do you mean?"

"Well, listen, Mother, I had scarcely passed by the barn when I noticed the ground was full of cracks, and knowing how I suffer from skin fissures, I wished to relieve this condition for the ground, so I applied the butter which I had in the dish; not having enough I went home for more and got what was in the small pail in the dairy. But still I did not have enough to fill all the cracks."

"Unfortunate child! Could one be more stupid? Has one ever heard of such a thing? You are going to catch a good whipping. It will teach you a lesson." She gives him a good switching and, to boot, sends him to bed without supper.

Another time she told him to make the bread and to be sure to make good bread. "Yes, Mother," he answered.

His mother out, he climbs to the attic to get a sack of flour, picks up a small pail to get water from the stream. But on the way he says to himself: "I am very foolish to carry water. Rather I shall carry the flour to the stream and mix it there in the stream."

He gets the flour and carries it to the stream, pouring a pailful into the water. One can just imagine he did not get a chance to mix it. The current was so swift that it carried it off. He kept on pouring the flour until there was none left; then sorrowfully for having failed, he returns home and hides.

His mother comes in, looks everywhere, but sees neither bread nor boy. She calls him, she looks for him and finally finds him under the bed. She makes him come to her and asks him to show her the bread.

"Don't mention it. I did not succeed. In order to save time, I carried the flour to the brook, but as soon as I poured flour in the water it would drift down the brook. I used all the flour without making dough, but it isn't my fault." He deserved a switching, did he not? His mother gave it to him and sent him to bed without supper.

Some time later she said to Foolish John: "I have to go to town. You will make the soap. I have put the ingredients in the pot. You will have to watch until it is boiled enough. This time try not to be stupid and blunder." "All right, Mother! But how will I know when it has boiled enough?" "When you will see the 'jelly' form on the rim of the pot, it will be time for you to add the salt and to stir it well until it gets thick and grainy; then it will be done. Have you understood me, son?" "Very well, Mother, don't worry. I shall make good soap." He starts stirring the soap with the paddle and his mother leaves for the village after having kissed him.

Foolish John stirs the soap a good while, but does not see the "jars" [pun]. He is tired and decides to call the gander. He calls "Piroche! Piroche!" but the gander does not show up. Then he goes around the outhouses, but does not see him. He decides to get the goose instead, so he goes to the stable where his mother had set the goose on eggs, catches her by the neck and dumps her in the boiling soap. A few minutes later he decides that the soap is done, and he removes the fire from around the pot and goes to play.

Suddenly he remembers the eggs and thinks that if the gander has not taken care of them, they will not have goslings this year. He runs to the stable and finds the eggs cold. "If I took the goose's place, it would do just as well." He sits on the eggs. Just imagine the fine omelet as a result, and the condition he was in! He stood up, such a mess! What was he going to do? He thinks of his dog, and calls: "Tontaine! Tontaine! Come lick my buttocks." To make it brief, he gets another whipping when his mother finds out about his tricks.

Much later, the mother, having to go to the village very early, says to Foolish John: "The only thing I want you to do today is to look after your grandmother. After she gets up, you will help her to bathe and then serve her breakfast." "Yes, Mother, don't worry; I shall take good care of Grandmother."

After the mother leaves, Foolish John heats the water, and having filled a large tub, he goes to look for his grandmother and finds her up and dressing. He tells her that he will give her a good hot bath before serving her breakfast. The old woman does not wish to hear about it, but Foolish John insists. He picks her up and places her in the hot water in spite of her terrible screams. He bathes her, using sweet-smelling soap, then with much difficulty, takes her out and places her in a chair after putting on her a pretty white jacket. She neither cries nor talks. "Grandmother, you must be feeling better. You smell very sweet.

I am going to prepare breakfast, wait a while." He leaves the room and soon returns with a tray full of food. "Here, dear Grandma, I brought you good chicken. Eat; it will do you good." He insisted in vain. The old woman neither said anything nor touched anything. He picked up a "drumstick" and placed it in her hand. Then he told her to eat it and he went outside to play, promising to return after while.

His mother came in at noon and Foolish John ran to tell her that he had given his grandmother a good hot bath although she did not want it. "When I dressed her she made faces, she was so happy. She did not want to eat, but I gave her a chicken leg and she went to sleep holding it in her hand."

"I am very pleased with you. I am going to ask your grandmother if it is true." She found her dead! Foolish John had scalded her.

The policemen took charge of him and put him in jail where he is to this day.

23

POT BELLY, BIG MOUTH
AND SKINNY LEGS

Once there were three men: Pot Belly, Big Mouth and Skinny Legs. They went to the woods to look for a plum tree. They found one. So Pot Belly climbed up the tree and ate plums until he "bust." Big Mouth laughed until he split his mouth, and Skinny Legs ran and stumbled on an ant and broke both legs.

24

THE KING'S JEWEL

THE PRINCESS HAD LOST HER DIAMOND and was in despair. The king promised a pile of money to the one who could tell where the diamond was. One day an old man by the name of Johnny the Shrewd arrived. He told the king that he knew where the diamond was, and if he promised to give him three meals, he would tell him. So after breakfast, Johnny the Shrewd said: "This is one [meal] I got." The servant began to tremble. After dinner, Johnny the Shrewd said: "This makes two [meals] I got." The servant was more nervous and trembled more. After supper, Johnny the Shrewd said: "This makes three I got." When the three servants who had stolen the diamond heard this, they fell on their knees and promised to return the diamond if he did not tell the king.

So Johnny the Shrewd went to tell the king that the diamond was in the duck's crop. Sure enough, that is where they found it.

Johnny the Shrewd collected his thousand dollars and left.

THE CUNNING OLD WIZARD
OR
JEAN MALIN

THERE WAS ONCE A PRINCE who was very rich. One day the princess, his daughter, lost a big diamond. While she was crying for her jewel, an old man came to the palace, and said that he was a wizard. The prince promised that he would give him anything he would ask, if he would say where was the diamond. The wizard only asked for three meals, and promised to find the jewel. They gave him an excellent breakfast, and when he had eaten all, he said: "One is taken." The servants of the prince began to tremble, because it was they who had stolen the diamond. After his dinner, the wizard said, "Two are taken." The servants trembled still more. After supper, the wizard said, "Three are taken." When they heard that, the three thieves fell on their knees before the zombie (wizard), and said that they would give back the diamond if he promised to say nothing to their master.

Now, the wizard took the diamond, rolled it up in a piece of bread, and threw it before a turkey in the yard. The turkey gobbled up the bread with the diamond. The wizard went to get the prince and his daughter, and told them that the diamond was in the turkey's stomach and that they would find it on killing the turkey. That was done, and the diamond was found. The prince was very glad, and said that the old man was the greatest wizard in the world. At the court everybody was admiring the wizard, but a few young men were not sure that he was a true wizard, and they wanted to catch him. They caught a cricket in the grass. They put it in a box, and they asked the wizard to tell them what there was in the box. The old man did not know, and he said to himself: "Well, Cricket, you are caught." His name was Cricket, but the people there did not know that, and they thought that the wizard had guessed that there was a cricket in the box. Therefore, the old man passed for a great wizard, and they gave him many good things, and yet, he was merely cunning, and had had luck.

24*b*: CANADIAN VARIANT

CRICKET IS CAUGHT

ONCE UPON A TIME a husband and wife by the name of Cricket lived in dire poverty. The wife held her husband responsible for this state of affairs, and nagged him daily for the future as well as the past since there were no prospects of a better life for them. She reminded him often that with a little schooling he could have obtained a position that would have meant a more agreeable existence.

One day the old man decided to go to school, and at the end of two weeks, finding the process too slow, gave up everything. Nevertheless an unusual occurrence happened during his school days. One night two travelers had stopped at the couple's home for lodging. The next morning after their departure, old Cricket went to the woods for an armful of firewood, where he found a small chest full of money, doubtless fallen from the carriage of the travelers. He hurried home to show it to his wife, who was very happy to have at last such a sum of money in their possession.

A short time later the two travelers returned to ask if the couple had not found a small chest. The old man, knowing that his wife had already spent some of the money, murmured in a low voice: "To be sure, Cricket is caught." The travelers asked

again, "Have you found a small chest of money?" "Well, yes,"
answered the old man. But the old woman hurriedly added:
"Gentlemen, do not pay any attention to this old fool. He does
not know what he is saying." "When did you find the chest of
money?" persisted the travelers.

"Oh well, it was when I attended school," he answered. "Do
not listen to him. Don't you see he is talking nonsense?" To
the great pleasure of the old woman, the travelers left. She made
great plans with the money so timely come to her. But she kept
on nagging her husband for having talked too much. Tired and
impatient, Cricket decided one night to get away. He left without saying a word to his wife, who, after all, did not care, since
she could get along without him now.

Upon arriving at the first village, Cricket, remembering that
his wife had often told him that he would make a good fortune
teller, had a sign made with the words: "I am the famous
fortune teller."

With this poster on his back, he went to the big city, capital
of the kingdom, where he hoped to make an honest living by
means of his profession. Upon arriving, he learned there was
much excitement in the city. The pretty princess of the king,
the eldest member of the family, had lost a precious pearl of
great value. She was so upset that it was feared she would lose
her mind. The king, on learning that there was a famous fortune
teller in town, sent his servants to get him. Cricket trembled with
fear and murmured: "Cricket is caught, to be sure."

The king called him and said: "You are the great fortune
teller. Well, you will have to tell within three days where the
precious pearl stolen from the princess is. If not, you will be
hanged at the door of the chateau."

The king had a room prepared for him and gave orders that
he should be watched. "Cricket is really caught," murmured
the latter as he walked to his improvised jail.

At the end of the first day, Cricket sadly went to the king
and asked him how many servants he had in the chateau.
"Three," answered the king. "Your honor, my king," said Cricket,

"tomorrow you will send your servants in turn, one to serve my breakfast, one for my dinner and the third for my supper." "Good," answered the king. "It will be done as you wish."

So the next morning his breakfast was served by the first servant. The meal was so good that Cricket could not help but tap his stomach and say while looking seriously at the servant: "Fine, this is one [meal] taken."

It is well to explain here that the precious pearl had been stolen by the three servants and the presence of the famous fortune teller in the chateau was not without causing them much worry. The least gestures or words of the fortune teller put them in mortal terror.

When the fortune teller, after having eaten his good meal, cried while looking at the servant: "Here is one taken," the servant went straight to his pals and told them the exact words of the fortune teller.

At noon the same scene took place. After enjoying his good meal, Cricket tapped his stomach and said: "Here is another taken." The servant hastened to tell his pals, not once thinking that the words referred to the meal. The same thing happened at supper time. The fortune teller tapped his stomach and uttered these words: "Well, I have had a good day. I have taken [had] three good ones [meals]." The third servant, frightened, went to tell his accomplices that the fortune teller was a sorcerer and would have them arrested. The best course would be to go see him and come to an agreement before the king learned of their crime.

So they went to see Cricket and promised him a thousand dollars cash and the precious pearl if he would not report them to the king. He accepted the proposition and promised to drop the case.

After this interview Cricket cried happily: "Well, that was not bad for the first experience!"

But it was necessary to return the jewel without incriminating the servants. So the next morning Cricket went out early and saw a large turkey among the chickens in the yard. He conceived the plan to mix the jewel with the feed or grain for the turkey. Soon the turkey had swallowed all, to the great satisfaction of Cricket.

At two that afternoon the king called a meeting of his family, his servants and a few policemen. He sent for the famous fortune teller to question him on the disappearance of the pearl. In answer to the first question, Cricket said: "Your majesty, I know very well where the pearl is. That beautiful turkey in your poultry yard swallowed it. I hesitated to tell you because I hate to see it killed."

"Indeed," said the king, "if you make me kill my beautiful turkey and we do not find the jewel, you will be punished severely." The king and the court went to the yard and the servants were ordered to wring the turkey's neck. In a short time the turkey was killed and opened. A cry of surprise was heard when the servants held the pearl so that all could see it.

The king was so impressed with the fortune teller's science that he gave him a purse full of money, had him dressed as a nobleman and ordered his servants to prepare one of the best rooms in the chateau for him.

One day, a servant went to see Cricket about her love affairs. She was madly in love with a young man and wanted to know if he would marry her. He assured her that this event would take place in the near future and that she would be very happy. She was satisfied, but wished to test further the fortune teller and see if he was really a sorcerer.

The next day she got a cricket and placed it between two plates, then went to ask him to guess what was between the plates. Cricket, surprised, murmured: "Well, this time Cricket is caught for sure."

The servant, surprised, went away convinced that he was really a sorcerer.

One day, Cricket, homesick for his native village, asked the king for a vacation, which was granted him with the invitation to return and bring his wife with him.

The three servants were afraid of him and had a grudge against him for having taken the jewel from them, and for the thousand dollars he had collected from them. Upon learning that he was leaving, they decided to follow him and to test once more his gift and to rob him if possible. One of them, who was the king's shepherd, was to pursue the fortune teller. He went to the sheepfold, filled a small sack with sheep's dung, then returned to meet his companions and all three started to follow Cricket. The latter, seeing them come, did not suspect their plan. As he was at the edge of the woods, he was afraid and murmured: "For sure, you are caught, Cricket." A short distance from him the servants stopped and the shepherd approached closer and, wishing to know if he was really a fortune teller, asked: "Cricket, can you .guess what I have in my sack? . . ." "Good Cricket is caught!"

But suddenly he thought that he was wearing a nobleman's clothes and sword, and he turned and said: "You, shepherd, you should go clean your sheep's dung!" And, drawing his sword, he stood bold, upright, ready for them.

Upon hearing the word "dung," the three servants looked at each other, scared stiff, and said: "He is really a sorcerer and able to play a trick on us." They turned around and retraced their steps, leaving Cricket to continue on his way.

Cricket was given a hearty welcome at home, for his wife had no one to nag in his absence. The longer he waited the more he dreaded returning to the chateau, for he dreaded having hard cases to guess, and being caught as a cricket.

But an unexpected event occurred which was to be fatal to Cricket. A powerful monarch having declared war against the king, the latter sent for Cricket and commanded him to tell him if he would be victorious in the war he was forced to fight. Cricket, thinking that he was really caught this time, assured him that he would be victorious in a very short time. But at the end of three weeks the king's army was destroyed, and he had to sign a humiliating treaty of peace.

The king, very angry, took it out on Cricket. He had him imprisoned in the tower of the chateau. His neck, his wrists, and his feet were placed in bands of wood until he expired.

This was the way poor Cricket died.

The manner of his death was spread by the servants and ever since then, whenever anyone suffers an unexpected misfortune, the refrain is repeated: "He was caught [or is caught] as poor Cricket."

25

THE DROLL MAN

A YOUNG OLD MAN had good eyes and good ears. While advancing he fell back, while being quiet, he was talking. He said he had seen a black streak of lightning, heard thunder without a sound. He was sitting standing, and lying down on his bed. He could never uncover his head without removing his hat. He had a boat, when it was on water it was not on land. He liked omelet, he wanted eggs in his omelet. He died on a Friday. If he could have lived until Saturday, he would have been a day older. He died with his head gently on an anvil. It would have been softer on a feather bed.

A droll man, a quarter of an hour before death, he was still alive.

26

THE TWO SHIPS

A COLD WAVE FROZE THE SEA and a captain shouted to another that a cold wave had frozen the ships. But he did not answer. The other shouted the same thing and did not get any answer either.

It made them angry. They began quarreling. The next day the sun came out, the ice melted, they were freed, they sailed and the frozen voices began to melt. The ships had left the place, but other ships passed them and heard them. They heard the quarrel, saw no one, heard lots of noise, but no one in sight. The frozen words were melting.

27

THE OLD BACHELOR

AN OLD BACHELOR was looking for the most stupid girl. He wanted to marry her. He walked and came to a house where there were an old man, an old woman, and an old maid. They lived in an old house with polypod on its roof.

The old man had a cow. He wanted to feed that grass to her, but he did not know how to go about it. So he told his wife that they would have to help him. He was to tie a rope around the animal's neck, climb on top of the house and pull her up while his wife and daughter would lift her until she would reach the polypod.

The old bachelor arrived at the house at that moment and wanted to know what they were doing. They explained that they were feeding the cow. "Well," he said, "why do you not break off the polypod and bring it down to the cow?" "Oh, yes," they replied, "we had not thought of it."

The old bachelor said to himself: "I must look further to see if there is someone more stupid. I shall walk farther." He did, and came to an old woman and a girl who had shelled some corn not dry enough to grind had placed it on the floor to dry, and were standing in the door trying to drive the sun on the corn.

The old bachelor arrived and said: "My goodness, what are you doing there?" "Well, we are drying the corn by driving the sun on it." He said: "Why don't you put your corn on a piece of cloth in the yard?" To himself, he mumbled: "This is stupid, but I must see if there is one more stupid."

He walked farther and saw a man and a woman in a house. He went in. Their daughter was lost. He joined them in looking for her. They found her crying behind the chimney. "Why are you crying?" asked the mother. "I am thinking of what I am going to do when I get married," she replied. "This is certainly the most stupid one in existence. I will not go any farther. I will marry her," he concluded.

28

THE FRUIT PEDDLER

THERE WAS A FRUIT PEDDLER who got on a steamer to cross the ocean. The captain objected to having him on board because he thought the fish would capsize his steamer in order to get the fruits, but he was assured that it would not happen, so the peddler was allowed to remain on board. While at sea, the fish got on. The captain grabbed the box of oranges and threw it overboard when he saw a big fish getting on. The fish swallowed the box and a little later came back for some more. This time the captain threw the basket of bananas overboard. The fish swallowed it, and returned later. This time they threw the peddler [Dago] overboard. The fish swallowed him too.

The ship reached land safely. A year later, fishermen caught the fish, cut him open without knowing the history of the fish. They found the Dago. He was sitting on the box of oranges, selling bananas at the same old price, two for a nickel. He had not changed his price.

29

MINETTE AND HER ROLLERS

MINETTE PLAYED AND LOST her rollers. She went to her mother for the keys. Her mother would not give her the keys without milk; she went to the cow for milk, the cow would not give her milk without hay; she went to the scythe for hay, the scythe would not give her hay without lard; she went to the sow for lard, the sow would not give her lard without acorns; she went to the oak for acorns, the oak would not give her acorns without wind; she went to the sea for wind. The sea gave her wind, the oak gave her acorns, the sow gave her lard, the scythe gave her hay, the cow gave her milk, her mother gave her the keys, and Minette got her rollers.

IV. ANIMAL TALES

30

BRER GOAT

BRER GOAT, BRER RABBIT, AND BRER TURTLE were in partnership to raise a crop. While the others were working, Brer Rabbit was scheming. He hollered loudly. Brer Goat asked him why he hollered. Brer Rabbit answered that someone wanted him to serve as godfather. Brer Rabbit went to get a drink out of a syrup can at the end of the row. When he returned, Brer Goat wanted to know if the child had been baptized and what the name was. Brer Rabbit responded the name was *Begun.*

A little later Brer Rabbit hollered again. Brer Goat wanted to know why. Brer Rabbit said it was another baptism. When he returned, Brer Goat queried him on the name of the infant. Brer Rabbit responded: *Halfway.* In a few minutes, Brer Rabbit hollered again. It was another baptism. When he returned, Brer Goat repeated the question about the infant's name. Brer Rabbit responded: *Finish.* He had finished drinking the syrup.

31

BRER TURTLE

BRER TURTLE WOULD STEAL Brer Goat's water with a gourd every night. He would say: "Gourd of water, gourd of water." When Brer Goat noticed this, he placed a tar baby at this well. Brer Turtle came as usual that night and said to the tar baby: "Good day, nigger." No answer. Brer Turtle said: "I'll slap you if you don't answer." He did, and his hand stuck. He repeated: "I am going to slap you again if you do not let me go." No answer. Brer Turtle slapped the tar baby with his other hand and it stuck too. Then he threatened to butt him with his head if he did not let him go. No answer, so he butted, only to get stuck again.

Next morning when Brer Goat went to the well, he saw Brer Turtle. He exclaimed: "So it was you stealing my water. Now, I am going to punish you." He gave him his choice of punishment; to be thrown in boiling water or the river. He cried: "In the pot of boiling water, because I would drown right away in the river." Brer Goat said: "In the river," but when Brer Turtle was in the river, he yelled: "I am at home."

32

THE HUNGRY BEAR

ONCE UPON A TIME a bear was passing by a hollow tree. He looked in it and saw a nest of wrens with five baby birds. He said: "It is not worth while." When the mother bird returned, the little birds told her what the bear had said. She replied that he would have to take it back. She ran after him, caught up with him and told him he had to take back what he said.

The wren proposed a battle. The bear asked her if she was ready. She replied that she would invite all flying animals and he would invite all the quadrupeds. They lined up for the battle. On one side the bear, the rabbit, and the fox; on the other side, the wren, the wasp, and the bumblebee. The rabbit was in front and asked for a flag to go to war. The fox replied that he could use his tail for a flag: Tail straight up would mean "fight," tail down, "surrender." The rabbit did not like this arrangement, but he accepted it anyway.

They went to the battlefield. The wasp added conditions and the fox gave his. The battle started. The third time the wasp stung the fox, he lowered his tail and the battle was over. The bear apologized to the wren for what he had said and the wren won the victory.

33

BRER RABBIT

Brer Rabbit was in the habit of stealing Brer Goat's vegetables. So Brer Goat set a trap for him in his garden. When Brer Rabbit was caught in the trap, he asked to be forgiven. Brer Goat refused to pardon him; instead, he built a big fire to burn Brer Rabbit. Then he asked him which he preferred for his punishment, to be thrown in the briars or in the fire. "Oh," replied Brer Rabbit, "I prefer the fire. The briars would scratch me too much." "Then," responded Brer Goat, "I shall throw you in the briars to punish you right. You stole all my vegetables." Brer Rabbit yelled when Brer Goat threw him in the briars: "I am at home."

PITI BONHOMME GODRON

(Tar Baby)

Alcée Fortier published this story in 1887 along with the translation reprinted here. In his introduction to the tale, he wrote:

This tale was written in 1884 by Mr. Zénon De Moruelle, of Waterloo, La., and communicated to me by my friend, Dr. Alfred Mercier. It is a genuine negro story, and illustrates admirably the peculiarities of speech and the quaint and sometimes witty ideas of our Louisiana negroes. With the author's permission, I now reproduce it from the manuscript, slightly modifying some expressions which appear to me a little too realistic, and changing the orthography to make it accord with my own ideas of the phonetics of the Creole patois, cf. Transactions of the Modern Language Association, 1884–85, page 103.

BONNEFOI, BONNEFOI; LAPIN, LAPIN!

I am going to relate to you something which is very funny, as you are going to see, and which happened a long time ago!

When the animals had the earth for themselves and there were yet but few people, God ordered them not to eat each other, not to destroy each other, but said that they might eat the grass with all kinds of fruits that there were on the earth. That was better, because they were all His creatures and it pained Him when they killed each other; but as quickly as they would eat the grass and fruits, He, God, would take pleasure to make them grow again to please them. But they did not obey the Master! Mister Lion began by eating sheep, the dogs ate rabbits, the serpents ate the little birds, the cats ate rats, the owls ate chickens. They began to eat each other. They would have destroyed each other, if God had not put a stop to all that!

He sent a great drought to punish their cruelty. It was a thing which was funny, nevertheless, as you are going to see.

There was smoke in the air, as when they burn cotton stalks; it looked as if there was a light mist. After sunset the heaven remained red like fire. The sea, the rivers, the lakes all began to fall, to fall; all fell at the same time, until there was not a drop of water remaining. Neither did the dew fall early in the morning to moisten the grass. Ah! I tell you, my friends, all animals found themselves in a great trouble. They were roaming about everywhere; their tongues were hanging out; they became thin.

There was among them a doctor who was called Mister Monkey, he was half wizard, half voodoo. They said he knew a great deal, but he was a big talker, and did very little. He said to the other animals that it was because they had made so many sins that God sent them all these misfortunes to punish them, that if there were any among them who wanted to pay, he would pray to make the rain fall. He had already succeeded very often when he asked for something; God in heaven always listened to *his* prayer. There was also a famous thief there, it was Mister Fox, who ate all the chickens there were in the neighborhood! He said to the other animals: "Don't you listen to Dr. Monkey, he is a d . . . rascal, he will take your money without giving you anything for it. I know him, he is a rascal, you will have no rain at all! It is better that we should dig a well ourselves. We need not count upon anything else. Let us go! Hurrah! Right off, if you are all like me, for I am very thirsty." Then Mister Monkey told him: "I think indeed that you are hungry, you d . . . pirate, now that you have finished eating all the chickens there were here, you are coming to play the braggart here." Mister Fox told him: "You are a liar, you know very well that the owls, the polecats and the weasels are eating all the chickens, and you come and say it is I. You know that if there is a thief here, it is you, you d . . . prayer merchant." All the other animals, tigers, lions, wolves, elephants, crocodiles, serpents, were running about to look for water. They had all assembled to hear the dispute of Dr. Monkey and Mister Fox.

I must tell you that if a hog grunts, a dog barks, a wolf howls, a cow bellows, each kind of animal has its own language. A tiger or an elephant or a lion cannot speak the language of another animal, each one speaks his own language, but when they are together, they all understand each other—the hog which grunts understands the dog which barks. It is not like us men, if a German comes to speak with a Frenchman or an American, he will not understand, any more than if an Englishman were to speak with a Spaniard who does not understand English. We men are obliged to learn the language of other nations if we want to converse with them. Animals are not at all like that, they understand each other as if they spoke the same language.

Well, I must tell you that Mister Fox pretended that if there was such a drought, the rain not having fallen for a year, so that all the grass was parched up, and the trees had lost their leaves, and there were neither flowers nor fruits, it was because there were no clouds in the heaven to give water, and not a prayer could make the rain fall. "All the water has gone into the ground, we must dig a large well in order to have water to drink. Listen to me, my friends, and we shall find water."

Lion, who was the king, opened his mouth, he roared, the earth shook, he spoke so loud! He beat his sides with his tail, and it made a noise like a big drum in a circus. All the other animals lay flat on the ground. He said: "By the very thunder, the first fellow who will speak to me about prayers, I shall give him something which will make him know me. I am a good fellow, when did I ever eat another animal? It is a lie, and I say that the little lawyer Fox is a fine little fellow. He is right, we must dig a well to have water immediately. Come here, Compair Bourriquet (Donkey), it is you who have the finest voice here; when you speak, it is like a soldier's trumpet. You will go everywhere to notify all animals that I, the king, I say that they must come to dig up and scratch the earth, that we may have water. And those that don't want to work, you will report them. You will come right off that I may compel them to do their share of the work or pay some other animal to do it."

Bourriquet was so glad he was to act as a newspaper, that he began to bray so loud that it was enough to render anybody

deaf. "Depart, depart," said the king, "or I shall strike you." Then
Bourriquet reared, and thought he was doing something nice, he
was so proud that the king had confidence in him, and then
that gave him the opportunity to order the other animals to
come, in the name of Lion, the king. On starting, he put down
his head, then he kicked half-a-dozen times with both feet, and
made a noise which was as if you were tearing up a piece of
cotonnade. That is his way of saluting the company when he is
glad.

Now, all the animals which he met, he told them that if they
did not come immediately to dig up and scratch the ground to
make a well, surely King Lion would eat them up. They were
all so much afraid, that they all came, except Compair Lapin
who was gnawing a little piece of dry grass.

"Don't listen to what I tell you, remain there, and don't come
right off, you will see what the king will do with you." "I don't
care a d . . . for you and the king together, come both of you,
you will see how I'll fix you. You may go to the devil. Do I
drink? Where did I ever use water? Surely, that is something
new to me. You are a fool, donkey that you are, I never drink,
a rabbit never drinks. My father and my grandfather did not
know how to drink, and as I am a real rabbit, I don't use water!
Never did a rabbit have little ones without ears, you hear. If
any one heard you he might believe that I am a bastard. Go
away, you big ears, for if I take my whip, I shall show you your
road, and make you trot faster than you ever galloped in your
life. If you knew me as I know you, you would not have stopped
here, surely."

Bourriquet saw that he could do nothing, so he went away;
but he was not as proud as when he started to tell all animals
that the king ordered them to come to work. As soon as he
arrived near the king, he said: "Master, I went on all your
errands, I saw all the animals in the world, only Compair Lapin
does not want to listen to reason. He says he does not need
water, let those who need it look for it. Besides, if you are not
satisfied, he will make you trot. You have no right to command
him, he is free, free as air, he has no master, none but God."

When the king heard that, he told a Tiger, who was there, to go with the Bear to arrest Compair Lapin and bring him here. "Take care you don't eat him on the way, for if you do, I'll give you such a beating as you never had before. You hear? Well, go!"

They started, and travelled a good while before they arrived. During this time, all the animals were working hard, each one had his share of the work, and they had even left a big piece as Compair Lapin's task, and that of the two who had gone to arrest him. They looked everywhere: in the prairie, on the mountain, at last they fell on Compair Lapin, who was eating the root of a cocklebur which was full of water. You know that rabbits know how to dig up the earth and find water below, in the roots.

At the same moment that they arrived near him, Compair Lapin was singing a little song which he had made about the king. He said in it that the king was a fool, and did not know how to govern, for his wife had many husbands and he was laughing to himself, and that perhaps, after they finished to dig that well, the king would make all the animals pay taxes to drink the water from the well they had dug with their sweat. "I am not so foolish, I am not going to work for that fellow! Let the others do it, if they are fools, I don't care any more for the king than a dog for Sunday. Tra la la," etc. . . . The Tiger approached without making any noise, and then he said: "Good morning, Compair Lapin, I ask your pardon, if I disturb you, but I don't do it on purpose; the king has ordered me to arrest you, I must obey him. You know that the weak must submit to the strong, this is why I advise you not to resist, because the Bear and I will be obliged to eat you. Take my advice, come quietly, perhaps you will come out all right! Your mouth is sweet, you will get Mister Fox to defend you; he is a good little lawyer and does not charge dear! Come, let us go."

When Compair Lapin saw that he could not do otherwise, he let the officers of the king arrest him. They put a rope around his neck, and they started. When they were near the dwelling of the king, they met Dr. Monkey on the way. He said: "Compair

Lapin, I think you are a pupil of Mister Fox, you will have to pay for it; you are gone up, my old fellow. How are you now? Don't you feel something getting cold within you. That will teach you to read the newspaper and meddle in politics on Sundays, instead of going quietly to mass!"

Compair Lapin answered briefly: "I don't care a d . . . for anything you say, old Monkey! And, then, you know, he who must die must submit to his fate. Just hush up, you rascal! You are trying to injure me, but perhaps you will be the loser; I have not given up all hope; perhaps, before long, you will be in trouble. Each one his chance; that is all I have to tell you."

At last, they arrived at a big tree which had been thrown down by the wind, and where the king was seated. The Tiger and the Bear, the two officers who were leading Compair Lapin, said to the king: "Here is the fellow!"

"Haw! Haw!" said the king, "we shall judge him immediately." Mister Fox came slyly behind Compair Lapin, and told him in his ears: "When they will ask you why you spoke badly of the king, say that it is not true, that it is Bourriquet who lied to do you harm. And then, flatter the king very much, praise him and make him some presents, you will come out all right. If you do what I tell you, you will find it well for you. Otherwise, if you are foolish enough to say all there is in your heart, take care, you will come out all wrong. I assure you that the king will make hash with you."

"You need not be afraid, Mister Fox, I know what I have to do; I thank you for your good advice; I am a lawyer myself."

Compair Lapin had suspected that they would come to arrest him as he had spoken so badly of the king and the government. It is for that he had put on his best coat, and a big gold chain around his neck. He had said to one of his neighbors with whom he was quite intimate, and also with his wife and daughter, and who was called Compair Bouki, when the latter asked him where he was going so finely dressed: "Yes, Compair Bouki, I shall soon go to see the king, and, as it is the coat that makes the man, this is why I dressed so well. It always produces a good effect on proud and foolish people."

When the king was ready to begin the case of Compair Lapin, he said to the policemen: "Bring the prisoner here to be judged."

Then Compair Lapin advanced, and said: "O Lion, my dear Master, you sent for me; here I am. What do you want?"

The Lion said: "I have to condemn you because you are always slandering me, and besides, you don't want to work to dig the well, which we are making to drink. Everybody is working except you, and when I sent Bourriquet to get you, you said to him, that I was a scoundrel, and that you would whip me! You will know that if your back has tasted of the whip, I have never been whipped; even my late mother did not dare to touch me! What do you have to say? You rascal with the long ears hanging down. I suppose they are so long, because the hounds have chased you so often. Speak right off, or I shall mash you, like a too ripe persimmon."

Compair Lapin kept quite cool; he knew that all that was a big wind that would bring neither rain nor thunder. He rubbed his nose with both paws, then he shook his ears, he sneezed, and then he sat down and said: "The king is justice on earth—as God is just in His holy Paradise! Great King, you who are more brave than all of us together, you will hear the truth. When you sent Bourriquet to get me, he who is more of a donkey than all the donkeys in the world, when he came to my house, I was sick. I told him: 'You will tell the king that I am very sorry that I cannot come now, but here is a fine gold chain, which you will present to the king for me, and you will tell him that I have forty twelve other animals to work in my place. Because that is too necessary a thing, to get a well; it is life or death for us, and we cannot do without it. Tell him also that there is but a great king like him to have such an idea, and enough brains to save us all!' What do you think he answered me? He replied that he did not care about a gold chain, that he did not eat that. If I had given him a basket of corn or some hay, he would have eaten it, but as to the chain, perhaps the king would hitch him up to the plow with that same chain, and he would be sorry to have brought it. When he went away, he said to me: 'Go on, Papa, I shall arrive before you, you will know that the ox which

is ahead always drinks clear water!' I suppose he meant that he
would speak before I should have the chance to be heard! As
I want the king to believe that I am not telling stories, I have a
witness who was there, who heard all our conversation. If the
king will have the kindness to listen to his testimony, he will
hear the same thing I have just told him." Compair Lapin bowed
to the king, and put the gold chain around Lion's neck, and then
he sat down on one side smiling, he was so sure that his gift
would produce a good effect and help him to come out all right
from his trouble.

Now, Lion said to Mister Fox to speak quickly. "I know all
that business, and if you come here to lie, I'll break your neck.
You need not wag your tail and make such grimaces, as if you
were eating ants. Come on, hurry! I have no time."

"Dear Master Lion," said the Fox, "I shall tell you how all
that happened: Compair Lapin, whom you see here, is the best
friend you have. The proof of it is that he brought a big chain
to make you a present. You will never see a Bourriquet do that;
that is sure, because there is not in the world a greater clown
than those donkeys. Dan Rice took twenty-one years to train a
donkey! He says that for $100,000 he would not undertake again
such a job. He would prefer to train fifty twelve thousand Lions,
because they would eat him up, or he would do something good
with them. Well, I must tell you, Mr. Lion, you, who are the
king of all animals, that same Bourriquet, whom you sent to
represent you, came to lie on you, and as to Compair Lapin, he
is as white as snow! Although Dr. Monkey has your confidence,
it is he who is governing secretly and advising all your people,
and putting them in rebellion against you the king to establish
another government, where that same Dr. Monkey and Bourriquet will govern in your place, when they will succeed in putting
you out. That is what they have been trying to do for a long
time, and that is what Compair Lapin and I wanted to tell you."

When the king heard that, he said: "That is all right; I am
glad you told me so. You can go with Compair Lapin, I acquit
him." But while they were hearing the case, Dr. Monkey and
Bourriquet thought that it was not healthy for them to remain

there, so they escaped when they saw that the wrong side was being warmed up. They vanished, and no one knew where they had gone, so well were they hidden. After that, Compair Lapin and Mister Fox both remained in the same parish where the king resided. Mister Fox was his deputy or chief clerk, and the other was mate, that is to say, he commanded the others and made them work to finish digging the well with their paws.

At last, the well was completed! All the animals drank, and they became strong again. The lioness recovered her health also, and some time after that, she gave birth to twelve little cubs as yellow as gold, and all as pretty as could be. The king was so glad that he pardoned all that were in the penitentiary, and he allowed the exiles to return. When he granted their pardon, he told them all to go and drink the water of the well. Then, you may imagine that Dr. Monkey with his accomplice Bourriquet came out of their hole to mingle with the others. But they began to spy and to watch all that was being done or said.

One day, they met Mister Fox, who was speaking of the government affairs in order to increase the tax. He and Compair Lapin found that there was not enough money in the treasury for them to become rich quickly. When Dr. Monkey saw them both together, he began to smile. He came near them, he bowed and said: "Let us forget what has passed, we must not be looking for those old papers. Let us be friends and live quietly like good neighbors." You might have thought they were the best friends when they parted. Dr. Monkey said to his partner Bourriquet: "You see these two fellows Compair Lapin and Mister Fox, they are d . . . scoundrels. I must get the best of them, or they will beat me; that is all I know!"

As Compair Lapin had said, when they judged him, that he never drank water, the king had told him: "Take care that you never try to drink water from this well, I want to see if you say the truth, and I order every one to watch you."

You will not believe me when I tell you that it is true that rabbits never drink water, there is always enough water for them in the grass which they eat. But expressly because they had forbidden Compair Lapin to drink from that well, he wished to do it. All the other animals praised that water so highly: it was so clear, so good. That gave him such a thirst, that he felt at every moment as if he had eaten well peppered salt meat. He said to himself: "I don't care a d . . . ; I shall drink, and I shall see who is going to prevent me. Besides, if they catch me, I shall always have the daughter of the king to protect me. She will find some way of preventing them from troubling me, for she has much influence with her father." He did as he said; every evening he drank his fill. But at last, he wanted to drink in the daytime also. It was a strange well; its water was not like any other water, it made people drunk like whiskey, only, instead of making you sick after you were drunk, it made you much stronger than before, and they were beginning to perceive that all those who were old were growing young again. Even the vegetables which you watered with it, if you cut them, the next day they would grow as fine as the day before.

When Compair Lapin began to see the effect of that water, he said: "I must have some for the day also, it does me a great deal of good, and as I am much older than the daughter of the king, I must become as young as she. Let me be, I shall arrange it. Don't you say anything." Well, when it was dark, he took his little calabash, which contained about two bottles of water, he went to the well, and filled it up. But he was so careful that the guard, which they put every evening near the well, saw nothing.

Dr. Monkey and Bourriquet watched all the time, because they could not forget how Compair Lapin had treated them whilst he was being judged. Therefore, they had sworn that they would catch him. But in spite of all their efforts, they wasted their trouble and their time. At last, one day, Dr. Monkey went to see Bourriquet, his comrade, and told him: "Come to my house, I have something to show you." He showed him Ti Bonhomme Godron (a man made of tar) and said: "It is with that I want to catch the fellow; as this time I shall be able to prove that he is guilty, we shall have all his money which the king will confiscate to give us for discovering all his rascalities.'

They took Ti Bonhomme Godron and put him in a little

path, where Compair Lapin was obliged to pass, very near the water. Then they started; they knew it was not necessary to watch; Ti Bonhomme Godron would attend to him without needing anybody's help. I know not if Compair Lapin suspected something, but he came quite late that evening. He never came at the same hour, but he managed things so well that he always got his water, and no one could catch him.

When he arrived the evening that they had placed Bonhomme Godron there, he saw something black. He looked at it for a long time. He had never seen anything like that before! He went back immediately, and went to bed. The next evening he came again, advanced a little closer, looked for a long time, and shook his head. At that moment, a frog jumped in the water *Tchoappe*. Compair Lapin flattened on the ground, as if crushed, and in two jumps he reached his house. He remained there days without returning, and Dr. Monkey and Bourriquet were beginning to despair, and to believe that it was true that Compair Lapin did not drink at all. But it was enough for this one that as it was forbidden him, he would be still more anxious to drink. "Oh! well," said he, "I don't care! I have some money here, but the remainder is hidden in the briars. If they catch me, I shall pay the police, and they will let me go. Besides, I have the protection of the daughter of the king; every night, she comes to see me. It would be very strange, if she did nothing for me. Besides, I have always instructed the police to let go a man who had money, and I suppose that they will make no exception for me, for they would lose the money which I will give them."

This reassured him. He started in the evening; it was a beautiful moonlight night, and every one was out late promenading. It was the end of spring: the honeysuckle perfumed the air, the mockingbird was singing in the pecan tree, there was a light breeze, which caused the leaves of the trees to dance, and the rustle prevented any one from hearing him walk. Everybody was in bed, only the dogs, from time to time, were barking at the big clouds, which were fleeing before the wind. "It is my turn now; I, Compair Lapin, I am going to drink, but a drink that will count." He took his calebash. When he arrived at the place where Bonhomme Godron was, the old fellow was still there. It had been warm during the day, and the tar was soft. When Compair Lapin arrived there, he said: "Hum, Hum, you have been long enough in my way. I do not come to drink, that is a thing which I never do, I want to take a bath to-night; get away from here. You don't want to answer? I tell you that I want to take a bath, you black scoundrel." Bonhomme Godron did not reply; that made Compair Lapin angry. He gave him a slap, his hand remained glued. "Let me go, or I shall strike you with the other hand." Bonhomme Godron did not reply. He struck him *cam* with the other hand; it remained stuck also! "I'll kick you, d . . . rascal, if you don't let me go." One foot remained stuck, and then the other one.

Then he said: "You are holding me that they might injure me, you want to try to rob me, but stop, you will see what I am going to do to you. Let me go, or I shall strike you with my head and break your mouth." As he said that, he struck, and a mule could not have hit harder, he was so mad. His head, however, my dear friends, remained stuck also. He was caught—well caught.

At daybreak, Dr. Monkey and Bourriquet arrived. When they saw Compair Lapin there, they laughed, they cursed him. They took a cart to bring him to prison, and all along the way they told the people how they had put a trap to catch the most famous rascal there was in the universe. It was the famous Compair Lapin who had so sullied the reputation of the king's daughter, that there was not a great prince who wanted to marry Miss Léonine, as Compair Lapin had spoken so much about his being her lover.

Master Fox, who was passing, heard all the bad things which Dr. Monkey and Bourriquet were saying about Compair Lapin, and he replied; "Yes, it is true, there is nothing like a thief to catch another thief."

When they were taking Compair Lapin to prison, all who passed on the road threw bricks at him, and they made a true clown of him. When he arrived in the presence of the king, the latter said to him: "Now, I would like to hear what you can say to get out of this scrape." Compair Lapin replied: "When the tree falls, the goat climbs on it! I know I can die but once, I don't care. If it is my money they want, I assure you that they will never see it. When I was free, never Bourriquet and Dr. Monkey tried to quarrel with me, the wild hog knows on what tree he must rub himself. I assure you that they are famous rascals."

"You must not speak in that way before the king, but the king will try your case in a few minutes."

"What I say is well said, I am ready to hear the judgment."

After the king and his friends had consulted together, they found Compair Lapin *guilty* and they condemned him to death. They ordered that he be put in prison until they could find an executioner willing to execute him. The king thought that he would get rid of a fellow who was too cunning for him, and then he would take vengeance on Compair Lapin, because he had injured Miss Léonine's character in such a manner that it was a scandal.

While Compair Lapin was in prison, he was thinking how he would manage to escape forever. He thought that he was in the worst plight than he had ever been before. He said to himself: "By Jove! that is no child's play. I think that I am gone up. Well, as I am tired, let me sleep a little: it will do me good." He lay down on the floor, and, soon after, he was snoring. He began to dream that the beautiful Léonine, the daughter of the king, was making a sign to him to tell him he need not be afraid, that she would fix everything all right.

He awoke contented, and at daybreak, the jailer opened the door of the prison and said to him: "They have found an executioner willing to execute you, but before that, they must cut off your ears; it is Bourriquet who has offered his services to send you in the other world. Take courage, my old fellow, I am sorry for you, you are a good fellow, but you risked your life too often. You know that an ounce of prevention is better than a pound of cure; now, it is too late. Good-bye, comrade."

At the same moment the sheriff came with his deputies to take him to the place of execution. They arrived at the steep bank of a little river. There were tall trees, grass, and briars everywhere. They chose a clear space. When they arrived, there was a big crowd: gentlemen, ladies, many children. All had come to see how they were going to kill Compair Lapin. The king was there with all his family. Miss Léonine, the daughter of the king, was there also. Oh! but she was so beautiful with her curls, which shone like gold in the sun. She had a muslin dress as white as snow with a blue sash, and a crown of roses on her head. The eyes of all were turned toward her; she was so pretty that they forgot completely Compair Lapin, who was trembling like a leaf. Yes, indeed, he was sorry to leave such a large fortune and such a beautiful wife as the king's daughter. What pained him the most was to think that perhaps Dr. Monkey or Bourriquet would marry Miss Léonine as soon as he would be dead. Because they both boasted that Compair Lapin was in their way. Without him, they said, they would have succeeded long ago.

Now, the king said: "Well, let us put an end to all this; advance Bourriquet, and read Compair Lapin his sentence." The king allowed him to choose his death, as he pleased: to be drowned in the river, burnt alive, or hung on a tree, or to have his neck cut with a sword.

"Yes, yes," said Compair Lapin, "all that at once, or one after the other, if that pleases you so much that I should die, well, I am very glad. Only, I was afraid that you would throw me in those great thorns, that would tear my skin and I would suffer too much, and then, the snakes and the wasps would sting me. Oh! no, not that, not that at all! Tell the king to do all except throwing me in those briars; for the love of God who is in Heaven, and who will judge you as you judge me!"

"Haw! Haw! you are afraid of the thorns? We want to see you suffer, suffer, you scoundrel."

They were making such a noise that the king said: "What is the matter?" He came closer, accompanied by Miss Léonine, who had come to see if Compair Lapin was going to die bravely; that is to say, everyone thought that, but she had come to encourage him and reassure him, because she had sent word to him secretly, while he was in prison, that even if the rope was around his neck, she, Miss Léonine, would arrive in time to take it off and save him, because she loved him more than anything in the world.

They related to the king and to Miss Léonine what Compair Lapin had said, and how much afraid he was to be thrown in the thorns and to suffer. Miss Léonine came forward and said: "Papa, I have a favor to ask you. I know that you hate Compair Lapin, and I also, because he has sullied my name. Well, I want to make you all see that what they said is not true. I want to see him suffer for all his stories. We must get rid of him, and I ask you to throw him in the briars and let him rot there; it is good enough for such a rascal." All clapped their hands, they were so glad.

"Throw him in the briars, it is there indeed we must throw him," said the king. "He must suffer. Quick! Hurry!" They took Compair Lapin by each limb, they swung him once; poor devil, he was crying: "No, no, not in the briars, in fire, cut my neck, not in the briars." They said: "Twice." *Vap!* they threw him in a great bunch of thorns.

As Compair Lapin fell in his native country, he sat down, he rubbed his nose, shook his ears, and then he said: "Thank you, all of you, I thought you were stupid, but it is here my mother made me; I am at home here, and not one of you can come here to catch me. Good-bye, I know where I am going." Miss Léonine also was very glad, she knew where she would meet Compair Lapin that very evening.

That proves one thing to you, that Compair Lapin was a hypocrite and pleaded false things to know the truth. It proves another thing, that when a woman loves a man, she will do all he wishes, and the woman will do all in her power to save him, and in whatever place the man may be, the woman will go to meet him. This is why they say that what a woman wants, God wants also.

As I was there when all that happened, they sent me here to relate it to you. I have finished.

CONCLUSION

ALTHOUGH LIMITED IN NUMBER, we think our collection of folk tales is comprehensive enough to show that the raconteur furnished a form of entertainment from the earliest settlement of French Canadians in Louisiana in the late seventeenth century until modern times, when he is being replaced by the radio and television. However, our folk literature, as all literature, contains gems of wisdom which are eternal. "Who will hang the bell around the cat's neck?" is as pertinent in the Space Age as it was in the Stone Age. Furthermore, recent research has proved that there is more unity in international folklore than in international politics.

MOTIF INDEX
OF THE TALES

ALTHOUGH FOLKLORE is as old as humanity, for centuries it was simply a form of entertainment—that is, an art. But the twentieth century has brought a big change in that science has become very important, and along with the new trend to analyze and classify everything, we have a system whereby we see the relationship of the folklore of all countries or cultures. Several scholars from all countries have contributed to this science. Among them is Stith Thompson, of Indiana University, whose learned work entitled *Motif-Index of Folk-Literature*, in six volumes (edition 1955–58), we have used for our index.

Thompson devised a plan to use letters of the alphabet for labeling chapters to classify different themes. For example, Chapter A concerns tales bearing on the creation of the world, etc.; B concerns animals; C is the chapter on taboos; etc., through Z, which lists those themes not included in preceding chapters. (He does not use I, O, and Y.)

Then in each alphabetical chapter there are subdivisions for which a decimal system is used. For example, in Chapter B, "Animals," B0 to B99 (mythical animals), we have the following divisions: B0–B9, mythical animals in general; B10–B19, mythical beasts; B20–B29, beast-men; B30–39, mythical birds; B40–B49, bird-beasts; B50–B59, bird-fish-beasts; B80–B89, fish-men; B90–B99, other mythical animals. Then a number are further subdivided, such as 19.1, 19.2, etc., to describe further analysis of the subject.

Themes in our tales are listed below according to this scheme—except, of course, the variants 22a, 24a–b, and 33a, which in general contain the same themes as the preceding.

stories with the same numbers. This list of themes is preceded by a classification of the tales according to the system of Antti Aarne in *The Types of the Folk-Tale* as translated and revised by Stith Thompson (Folklore Fellows Communication No. 74, 1928).

THE TALES CLASSIFIED
ACCORDING TO AARNE AND THOMPSON

Semi-legendary (Novelle)

1. GENEVIÈVE DE BRABANT. Type 870 with modifications.

Fairy Tales (Ordinary Folk Tales)

2. CINDERELLA. Type 510.
3. JULIE AND JULIEN. Type 313.
4. THE SEVEN-HEADED ANIMAL. Types 300, V; 302, I; and 326.
5. BEAUTY AND THE BEAST. Type 401, with elements of 425.
6. THE TURKEY RAISER. Types 314 and 531, with many modifications.
7. THE RISING WATER, THE TALKING BIRD AND THE WEEPING Tree. Type 706 with modifications.
8. THE MAN AND HIS SON. Type 325 (mixed).
9. THE MILLIONAIRE, HIS DAUGHTER AND HER THREE SUITORS. Type 513.
10. THE MAN AND HIS THREE SONS. Type 505 with elements of 566.
11. THE MILLER. Type 500, II and III.
12. MOUSTAFAT. Type 460B and 675.
13. POUCETTE. Type 327.
14. ROCLORE I. Types 1525 and 1590.
15. ROCLORE II. Types 1525 and 1590.
16. THE LITTLE BIRD. Type 780.
17. LITTLE JOHN I. Type 853 (mixed).

18. . LITTLE JOHN II. Type 314 (mixed).
19. LITTLE JOHN III. Type 313.
20. THE POOR MAN'S SON. Type 592.

Comical Tales (Jokes and Anecdotes)

21. THE HUNCHBACK. Types 1000 and 1004.
22. FOOLISH JOHN. Type 1210.
23. POT BELLY, etc. Type 1088.
24. THE KING'S JEWEL; or, CRICKET IS CAUGHT. Type 1641.
25. THE DROLL MAN. (Contradictions.) Type 2411.
26. THE TWO SHIPS. Type 1960, H.
27. THE OLD BACHELOR. Types 1210 and 1384.
28. THE FRUIT PEDDLER. Type 1960B.
29. MINETTE AND HER ROLLERS. Type 2030.

Animal Tales

30. BRER GOAT. Type 15 (goat substituted for fox).
31. BRER TURTLE. Type 175 (turtle substituted for rabbit).
32. THE HUNGRY BEAR. Type 222.
33. BRER RABBIT. Type 30, with modifications.

THEMES IN THE FOLK TALES

A. Mythological Motifs

A998.1. Origin of clay (dust). Tale 16.

B. Animals

MYTHICAL ANIMALS

B11.2.3.1. Seven-headed dragon. Tale 4.
B29.7. Man-bear. Tale 5.
B81. Mermaid. Woman with tail of fish, lives in sea. Tale 6.

MAGIC ANIMALS

B122.1.1. Birds tell a secret. Tales 3, 16.
B184.1.1. Horse with magic speed. Tales 6, 8, 18.
B184.1.4. Magic horse travels on sea and land. Tale 18.

ANIMALS WITH HUMAN TRAITS: SPEECH

B211.1.2. Speaking goat. Tale 30.
B211.2.3. Speaking bear. Tale 32.
B211.2.6. Speaking hare. Tale 33.
B211.3. Speaking bird. Tales 7, 16, 32.
B211.3.2. Speaking cock. Tale 3.
B211.3.2.1. Speaking chicken. Tale 3.
B211.3.10. Speaking eagle. Tale 3.
B211.7.3. Speaking amphibia (turtle). Tale 30.

HELPFUL ANIMALS

B301.1. Faithful animal at master's grave dies of hunger. Tale 1.
B301.8. Faithful lion follows man. Tale 4.
B392. Hero divides spoil for animals. Tale 3.
B392.1. Animals grateful for being given appropriate food. Tales 4, 6.
B401. Helpful horse. Tales 6, 18.
B431.2. Helpful lion. Tale 4.
B431.3. Helpful tiger. Tale 4.
B435.4. Helpful bear. Tale 4.

SERVICES OF ANIMALS

B524.1. Animals overcome man's adversary by force. Tale 4.
B535.0.15. Doe as nurse for child. Tale 1.
B548.2. Fish brings lost object from bottom of sea. Tale 6.
B563.2. Birds point out road to hero. Tale 3.

C. *Taboo*

C120.1.   Kissing forbidden. Tales 3, 19.

C600.1.   Unique prohibition. Removal of bridle from horse forbidden. Tale 8.

C610.1.   The one forbidden place—home. Tale 1.

C611.   Forbidden chamber. Tale 6.

C650.   One compulsory thing. Tales 1, 13, 21.

C740.1.   Act of courtesy forbidden. Tale 7.

C761.3.   Staying too long at ball. Tale 2.

C837.   Loosing bridle in selling man transformed to horse. Tale 8.

C912.   Hair turns to gold as punishment in Forbidden Chamber. Tale 6.

C963.   Person returns to original form when taboo is broken. Tale 2.

D. *Magic*

TRANSFORMATION

D20.   Transformation to person of different social class. Tale 2.

D25.1.   Transformation of layman to a doctor. Tales 8, 10.

D25.3.   Transformation of lay persons to altar boys. Tale 3.

D131.   Transformation of man to horse. Tale 8.

D136.   Transformation of man to swine. Tale 3.

D161.3.   Transformation of man to duck. Tale 3.

D170.   Transformation from man to fish. Tale 8.

D290.   Transformation of man to cloud. Tale 3.

D435.1.1.   Transformation statues come to life. Tale 7.

D521.   Transformation through wish. Tales 3, 6.

D535.   Transformation from man to horse by pulling on bridle. Tale 8.

D537.   Transformation by changing clothes. Tale 5.

D565.2.   Transformation by touching with rod. Tale 2.

D565.6. Transformation by touching water. Tale 7.
D610.   Repeated transformation. Tale 8.
D630.   Transformation and disenchantment at will. Tale 8.
D672.   Obstacle to flight. Tale 18.
D672.1. Magic objects as decoy for purser. Tale 19.
D683.2. Transformation by witch or sorceress. Tale 3.

DISENCHANTMENT

D722.   Disenchantment by taking off bridle. Tale 8.
D730.   Disenchantment by submission. Tale 5.
D766.1.1. Disenchantment by water and command. Tale 7.

KINDS OF MAGIC OBJECTS

D975.2. Magic rose. Tale 5.
D985.5. Magic fig. Tale 10.
D1023.5. Magic hair of horse's tail. Tale 6.
D1057. Magic belt. Tale 10.
D1065. Magic boots. Tale 19.
D1067.1. Magic hat. Tale 20.
D1072.1. Magic comb. Tale 19.
D1096.1. Magic gun. Tales 8, 20.
D1121.0.1. Boat made by magic. Tale 9.
D1195. Magic soap. Tale 19.
D1209.1. Magic bridle. Tale 8.
D1222. Magic horn. Tale 10.
D1233. Magic violin. Tale 20.
D1242. Magic fluid (sweat) of horse. Tale 6.
D1242.1. Magic water. Tale 7.
D1246. Magic powder. Tale 10.
D1254.1. Magic wand. Tales 2, 3, 12.
D1258.1 Bridge made by magic. Tale 12.
D1258.2 House made by magic. Tale 12.
D1273.1.1. Magic numbers. Tales 3, 4, 6, 7, 9, 10.
D1273.1.3. Seven as a magic number. Tale 6.
D1273.1.5. Eleven as a magic number. Tale 2.

CHARACTERISTICS OF MAGIC OBJECTS

D1393. Magic object (sponge) helps fugitive. Tale 19.
D1415.2.5. Magic fiddle causes dancing. Tale 20.
D1451. Inexhaustible purse furnishes money. Tale 10.
D1611.4. Magic beans (peas) answer for fugitive. Tale 19.
D1611.19. Magic pins on cork answer for fugitive. Tale 3.
D1615. Magic singing object. Tale 16.
D1641.4. Forest cleared by magic. Tale 19.

MAGIC POWERS AND MANIFESTATIONS

D1711. Magician. Tales 2, 3, 9, 12.
D1711.10.3.1. Grand Vizier (Turk). Tales 4, 6, 7.
D1720.1. Man given powers of wishing. Tales 3, 12.
D1721.1.2. Magic power from demon. Tale 8.
D1885. Rejuvenation by boiling (in lard). Tale 18.
D2003. Forgotten fiancée. Tales 2, 18.
D2004.2. Kiss of forgetfulness. Tales 3, 19.
D2174. Magic dancing. Tale 20.
D2183. Magic spinning. Tale 11.

E. The Dead

E300. Friendly return from the dead. Tale 10.
E341.1.1. Dead grateful for having been spared indignity to corpse. Kind man has given it burial. Tale 10.
E565. Ghosts clank chains (noise in cemetery and old church). Tales 4, 5.
E610.1. Reincarnation as man to horse to man. Tale 18.
E610.1.1. Reincarnation: boy to bird. Tale 16.
E632.1. Speaking bones of murdered person reveal murder. Tale 16.

F. *Marvels*

SPIRITS AND DEMONS

F402.1.4. Demons assume human form in order to deceive. Tale 11.

F402.6. Dwelling of demons. Tale 6.

F419.1. Demons hold horse race. Tale 8.

REMARKABLE PERSONS

F531. Giants. Tale 13.

F531.6.8.6. Giants have children. Tale 13.

F535. Pygmy. Remarkably small man. Tale 11.

F535.1. Tom Thumb (thumbling). Tale 13.

F535.1.1. Adventures of thumbling. Tale 13.

F545.1.1. Blue Beard. Tale 3.

F551. Remarkable feet. Tale 11.

F552.1. Hands with unusual fingers. Tale 11.

F555.1. Gold hair. Tale 6.

F561. People of unusual diet. Tales 1, 7.

PERSONS WITH SPECIFIC POWERS

F571. Extremely old person. Tale 9.

F577. Persons identical in appearance. Tale 13.

F601.7. Animals as extraordinary companions. Tale 4.

F613.3. Strong man's labor contract. Tale 21.

F641. Person of remarkable hearing. Tales 9, 17.

F652. Marvelous sense of smell. Tale 13.

F660. Remarkable skill. Tales 11, 24.

F661.10.1. Marksman grazes tip of nose. Tales 9, 17.

F679.7. Skillful gambler always wins. Tale 3.

F681. Marvelous runner. Tales 9, 17.

F699.1.1. Marvelous eater. Tale 9.

EXTRAORDINARY PLACES AND THINGS

F752.4.   Mountain of ice. Tale 26.

F814.1.1.   Gigantic flower (rose). Tale 5.

F823.   Extraordinary shoes. Tales 2, 19.

F931.4.   Extraordinary behavior of waves. Tale 26.

F935.3.   Extraordinary occurrences connected with bayou. Tales 3, 19.

F956.   Extraordinary diagnosis. Tale 10.

F981.6.   Animal dies of broken heart. Tale 1.

G. *Ogres*

CANNIBALS AND CANNIBALISM

G11.2.   Cannibal giant. Tale 13.

G30.   Person becomes cannibal. (Boy transformed eats devil transformed.) Tale 8.

G61.   Relative's flesh eaten unwittingly. Tale 16.

G84.   Fee, fi, fo, fum. Cannibal returning home smells human flesh. Tale 13.

GIANT OGRES

G100.1.   Giant ogre. Tale 13.

G111.   Giant ogres (devil) possess castle. Tale 6.

WITCHES

G202.   Beneficent witch. Tale 12.

G263.1.4.   Witch (devil) transforms husband into dog (horse). Tale 6.

G269.10.   Witch punishes person who incurs her ill will. Tale 9.

G284.   Witch as helper. Tales 3, 9, 12.

OTHER OGRES

G303.3.2.3.   Devil (helper) as a dwarf. Tale 11.
G303.6.1.5.   Devil appears when cards are played. Tale 19.
G303.7.1.1.   Devil rides black horse. Tale 6.
G303.9.2.   The devil performs deeds of unusual strength. Tale 19.
G303.9.7.   The devil advises human beings. Tales 6, 19.
G303.9.8.3.   Devil (dwarf) dances on grave (in fire). Tale 11.
G303.11.2.   The devil's son (godson). Tale 6.
G303 11.5.   The devil's daughter. Tale 19.
G303.16.19.13.   Devil cannot follow man over running water. Tale 6.

FALLING INTO OGRE'S POWER

G400.   Person falls into ogre's (Satan's) power. Tale 6.

OGRE DEFEATED

G530.   Ogre's relative aids hero. Tale 13.
G551.4.   One brother rescues another from ogre. Tale 13.

H. *Tests*

IDENTITY TESTS

H36.1.   Slipper test. Identification by fitting of slipper. Tale 2.
H105.1.   Dragon-tongue proof. Tale 18.
H105.2.   Tongue as proof that man has been murdered. Tale 1.
H110.   Identification by clothing. Tale 13.
H145.1.   Identification by hand. Tale 19.

MARRIAGE TESTS

H301.   Excessive demands to prevent marriage. Tale 19.
H326.   Suitor test: skill. Tales 4, 9.
H335.   Tasks assigned suitor. Tales 18, 19.

H335.0.1. Bride helps suitor perform tasks. Tales 3, 4, 6, 9.
H342. Suitor test: outwitting princess. Tale 17.

TESTS OF PROWESS: TASKS

H915.1. Task assigned because of man's boast. Tale 11.
H971. Task performed with help of old woman. Tale 9.
H972. Task accomplished with help of grateful dead. Tale 10.
H973.3. Task performed by dwarf. Tale 11.

NATURE OF TASKS

H1010. Impossible tasks. Tales 3, 11, 19, 21.
H1023.3.1.1. Task: procuring cuckoo to sing in winter. Tale 21.
H1092. Task: spinning impossible amount in one night. Tale 11.
H1129.2.1. Emptying and filling bedticks with feathers without losing one feather. Tale 19.
H1129.6. Task: clearing land. Tale 19.
H1132.1. Task: recovering lost object (clarinet) from sea. Tale 19.
H1137. Task: moving arms of sea. Tale 19.

TESTS OF PROWESS: QUESTS

H1210.2. Quest assigned by king. Tale 11.
H1219.1. Quest assigned as payment for gambling loss. Tales 3, 19.
H1233. Animals help hero on quest. Tales 3, 4, 6, 16.
H1235. Succession of helpers on quest. Tales 3, 4, 11, 17.
H1292.21. Who is my godfather? Tale 6.
H1311. Quest for the richest person. Tales 7, 9.
H1312.2. Quest for most stupid girl as bride for oneself. Tale 27.
H1317.1. Quest for ornament (diamond). Tale 24.
H1321. Quest for the fountain of youth. Tale 18.
H1376.2. Quest: learning what fear is. Tale 4.
H1386.5. Quest for lost rollers. Tale 29.

H1388. Quest: answer to certain question. (What is her name?) Tale 11.

FEAR TEST

H1412.1. Spending night in old church. Tale 4.

J. *The Wise and the Foolish*

ACQUISITION AND POSSESSION OF WISDOM (KNOWLEDGE)

J10. Wisdom acquired from experience. Tale 11.
J50. Wisdom acquired from observation. Tale 5.

WISE AND UNWISE CONDUCT

J227. Death preferred to other evils. Tale 5.
J229.12. Prisoners given choice. Tales 31, 33.
J230. Choice: real and apparent values. Tale 9.
J231. Choice between love and wisdom. Tale 4.
J264. Apparent beauty may be of the least importance. Tale 2.
J412.2. Choice of money or friends. One son chooses friends, two choose money. Tale 10.
J484. Enjoyment preferred to wealth. Tale 6.
J914. King shows humility by mingling with common people. Tale 7.
J962. Task performed by close observation. Tale 2.

CLEVERNESS

J1130. Cleverness in law court. Tale 20.
J1141.16. The thief is tricked into betraying himself in supposed ordeal. Tale 24.
J1179.10. Enoch Arden decision. Tales 3, 19.

FOOLS AND OTHER UNWISE PERSONS

J1860. Animal or object absurdly punished. Tale 23.
J1881.1.3. Three-legged pot sent to walk home. Tale 23.

J1902.1. Numbskull sits on eggs to finish the hatching. Tale 23.

J1930. Absurd disregard of natural laws. Tales 25, 26, 27.

J2079.3. Foolish wish to marry the most foolish girl. Tale 27.

J2200. Absurd lack of logic. Tale 27.

J2499. Literal fools. Tales 22, 27.

K. *Deceptions*

CONTESTS WON BY DECEPTION

K10. Athletic contest won by deception. Tales 9, 17.

K40. Labor contest won by deception. Tale 21.

DECEPTION IN PAYMENT OF DEBT

K221. Payment to be made at harvest (Christmas) time. Tale 20.

THEFTS AND CHEATS

K301. Master thief. Tales 14, 15.

K331.2.2. Guards fatigued by trickster so that they sleep while goods are stolen. Tales 14, 15.

K341. Owner's interest distracted while goods are stolen. Tales 14, 15.

K372. Playing godfather. Tale 30.

ESCAPE BY DECEPTION

K500. Escape by deception. Tales 14, 15.

K512.2. Compassionate executioner: substituted heart (tongue) of animal for heroine's. Tale 1.

CAPTURE BY DECEPTION

K700. Capture by deception. Tales 14, 15.

K741. Capture by tar baby. Tale 31.

K750. Capture by decoy. Tale 15.

K776. Capture by intoxication. Tale 14.

FATAL DECEPTION

K940.   Deception into killing own family. Tale 16.
K940.1. Man betrayed into eating his own children. Tale 16.
K1000.   Deception into self-injury. Tale 21.

SEDUCTION OR DECEPTIVE MARRIAGE

K1315.   Seduction by posing as magician. Tale 12.

DUPE'S PROPERTY DESTROYED

K1440.   Dupe's animals destroyed or maimed. Tale 21.

DECEPTION BY DISGUISE OR ILLUSION

K1611.   Substituted caps cause ogre to kill his own children.
  Tale 13.
K1714.2. Victim (king) tricked into large pot of boiling grease.
  Tale 18.
K1836.   Disguise of man in woman's dress. Tale 14.
K1892.1. Trickster hides in bag in order to be carried.
  Tales 14, 15.

IMPOSTURES

K1920.   Substituted children. Tale 13.
K1931.1. Impostors throw hero overboard into the sea. Tales
  14, 15.
K1955.   Sham physician. Tale 10.

HYPOCRITES

K2010.   Hypocrites pretend friendship but attack. Tales 1, 18.
K2115.   Animal-birth slander. Tale 7.

L. *Reversal of Fortune*

VICTORIOUS YOUNGEST CHILD

L10. Victorious youngest son. Tales 10, 11, 21.
L50. Victorious youngest daughter. Tales 3, 7.
L55.1. Abused stepdaughter. Tale 2.

UNPROMISING HERO (HEROINE)

L102. Unpromising heroine. Tale 2.
L111.2. Foundling hero. Tale 4.
L112.2. Very small hero. Tale 13.
L142. Pupil surpasses teacher. Tale 8.
L160. Success of the unpromising hero or heroine. Tale 11.
L161. Lowly hero marries princess. Tales 4, 6, 9, 12, 17.
L162. Lowly heroine marries prince. Tale 2.
L165. Lowly boy becomes king. Tale 15.

MODESTY BRINGS REWARD

L220. Modest choice best. Tale 5.

TRIUMPH OF THE WEAK

L300. Triumph of the weak. Tales 8, 21.
L310. Weak overcomes strong. Tales 18, 19, 20.
L330. Easy escape of weak. Tales 31, 33.

PRIDE BROUGHT LOW

L410. Proud ruler humbled. Tales 14, 15.
L430. Arrogance repaid. Tale 1.
L450. Proud animal less fortunate than humble. Tale 32.
L460. Pride brought low. Tale 2.

M. *Ordaining the Future*

JUDGMENTS AND DECREES

M2.   Inhuman decision of king (and of mother). Tales 1, 16.
M10. Irrevocable judgment. Tale 5.
M20. Shortsighted judgments. Tales 6, 7, 27.

VOWS AND OATHS

M151.2.   Vow not to marry until quest is concluded. Tale 4.

BARGAINS AND PROMISES

M210. Bargain with the devil. Tales 8, 20.
M291. Trickster undertakes impossible bargains and collects
his part. Tales 3, 14, 15.
M237. Bargain to save face. Tale 1.

PROPHECIES

M301.2.1.   Enraged old woman prophesies for youth. Tale 9.

CURSES

M412.1.   Curse given at birth of child. Tale 12.
M420. Enduring and overcoming curses. Tale 6.
M446. Undertaking dangerous quest. Tales 18, 19.

N. *Chance and Fate*

WAGES AND GAMBLING

N1.1.   Hero makes fortune through gambling. Tale 3.
N2.   Extraordinary stakes at gambling. Tales 3, 8.
N4.   Devil (Blue Beard) as gambler. Tales 3, 8.

THE WAYS OF LUCK AND FATE

N201. Wish for exalted husband realized. Tale 7.
N211.1.6. Lost diamond found in duck's gizzard. Tale 24.
N271.6.1. Child's (bird's) song reveals murder. Tale 16.

UNLUCKY ACCIDENTS

N320. Person unwittingly killed. Tale 13.

LUCKY ACCIDENTS

N475. Secret name overheard by eavesdropper. Tale 11.
N620. Accidental success in hunting. Tales 1, 7.
N680. Series of lucky successes. Tale 19.
N681. Husband (wife) arrives home just as wife (husband) is about to marry another. Tales 3, 19.

ACCIDENTAL ENCOUNTERS

N711. King (prince) accidentally finds maiden and marries her. Tales 2, 7.
N741. Unexpected meeting of husband and wife. Tale 1.

HELPERS

N811. Supernatural godfather. Tale 6.
N812.3.1. Grateful dead as helper. Tale 10.
N819.2. Transformed person as helper. Tale 6.
N821. Help from little man. Tale 11.
N825.1. Childless couple adopt hero. Tale 4.
N825.2. Old man helper. Tale 18.
N825.3. Old woman helper. Tale 13.
N825.3.2. Old woman by spring as helper. Tale 9.
N836. King as helper. Tale 7.
N845. Magician (sorceress) as helper. Tales 2, 12.
N857. Enemy's servant as helper. Tale 1.
N861. Foundling as helper. Tale 4.

P. *Society*

ROYALTY AND WEALTHY

P10.   Kings. Tales 1, 4, 6, 7, 10, 11, 12, 14, 15, 18, 21, 24.
P20.   Queens. Tales 7, 11, 14.
P30.   Princes. Tales 2, 5, 21.
P40.   Princesses. Tales 4, 6, 10, 11, 12, 17, 18, 24.
P50.   Noblemen (knights). Tale 1.
P60.   Noble (gentle) ladies. Tale 1.
P90.   Royalty and nobility (Grand Vizier). Tales 4, 6, 7.
P150.   Rich man. Millionaire. Tales 9, 20.

THE FAMILY

P210.   Husband and wife. Tales 1, 2, 3, 4, 13, 14, 16, 27.
P230.   Parents and children. Tales 1, 3, 4, 8, 9, 10, 11, 13, 16, 27.
P231.1. Boy sickens from grief at mother's death. Tale 1.
P231.3. Mother love. Tale 11.
P250.   Brothers and sisters. Tales 2, 3, 5, 7, 9, 10, 13, 16, 19, 21.
P262.   Mother-in-law. Tale 21.
P282.   Stepmother. Tale 2.
P284.   Stepsister. Tale 2.
P296.   Godparents. Tales 3, 6.

OTHER SOCIAL RELATIONSHIPS

P310.   Friendship. Tale 10.
P320.   Hospitality. Tales 2, 3, 5, 14.
P340.   Teacher and pupil. Tales 8, 18.
P360.   Master and servant (valets). Tales 1, 6, 8, 12, 14, 15, 24.

TRADES AND PROFESSIONS

P412.1. Shepherd. Tale 14.
P412.4. Hero as turkey-"herd." Tale 6.

P414. Hunter. Tale 18.
P421. Judge. Tale 20.
P424. Physician. Tale 8.
P426.1. Priest (parson). Tale 4.
P431. Merchant (street merchandise). Tale 18.
P443. Miller. Tale 11.
P448. Butcher. Tale 18.
P451. Spinner. Tale 11.
P456. Carpenter. Tale 9.
P458. Woodsman. Tale 9.
P461. Soldier. Tale 1.
P475. Robber. Tales 14, 15.

GOVERNMENT

P510. Law courts. Tale 20.
P512.2. Release from execution by clever trick. Tale 20.
P526. Legal principles. Tales 3, 19.
P551. Army. Tale 10.

CUSTOMS

P621. Bridle goes with horse when horse is bought. Tale 8.
P634.0.1. Customs connected with food. Tales 4, 7, 9, 16.

NATIONS

P711. Patriotism. Tale 1.

Q. *Rewards and Punishments*

DEEDS REWARDED

Q2. Kind and unkind. Tales 2, 3, 5, 9, 10.
Q32. Lion (man) divides slain bullock (dead man). Tale 4.
Q37. Reward for carrying out dead man's request. Tale 10.

NATURE OF REWARDS

Q51. Kindness to animals rewarded. Tales 4, 6.

Q53.3.2. Maiden gives her hand and riches to man who builds boat. Tale 9.

Q81. Reward for perseverance. Tale 11.

Q82. Reward for fearlessness. Tales 4, 5.

Q111. Riches as reward. Tale 8.

Q149. Miraculous or magic reward. Tale 20.

DEEDS PUNISHED

Q260. Deceptions punished. Tale 1.

Q263. Lying punished. Tale 4.

Q280. Unkindness punished. Tale 7.

Q321. Laziness punished. Tale 12.

KINDS OF PUNISHMENT

Q411. Death (hanging) as punishment. Tales 1, 4, 6.

HUMILIATING PUNISHMENT

Q429.1. Punishment: culprit (devil) eaten by cannibals. Tale 8.

Q429.3. Cutting into pieces as punishment. Tale 1.

Q438. Punishment: abandonment in forest. Tale 1.

Q451.8. Punishment: thong of leather (skin) cut from back. Tale 21.

Q458. Flogging and kicking as punishment. Tale 22.

Q467.1. Casting of king into water in sack. Tales 14, 15.

Q471.1. Persecuted queen meanly clothed and set where all are commanded to spit on her. Tale 7.

Q491. Indignity to corpse as punishment. Tale 1.

Q499.2. Humiliating death as punishment. Tale 19.

Q551. Transformation to stone as punishment. Tale 7.

Q552. Death by thunderbolt as punishment. Tale 16.

Q552.2.0.1. Quaking of earth as punishment. Tale 11.

R. *Captives and Fugitives*

CAPTIVITY

R4. Surprise capture of king. Tales 14, 15.

R18. Abduction by rejected suitor. Tale 1.

R35. Abducted princess gives birth to child. Tale 1.

R41.3. Captivity in dungeon. Tale 1.

RESCUES

R111.1.9. Princess (maiden) rescued from undeserving suitor. Tale 4.

R131.1. Hunter rescues abandoned child. Tale 1.

R135. Abandoned children find way back by clue (pebbles). Tale 13.

R135.1. Crumb (flour) trail eaten by birds. Lost person cannot find way back. Tale 13.

R151.1. Husband rescues stolen wife. Tale 1.

R153.3. Father rescues son. Tale 1.

R155.1. Youngest brother rescues his older brothers. Tales 10, 13.

R163. Rescue by grateful dead man. Tale 10.

R169.4. Hero (heroine) rescued by servants (valets). Tale 1.

R187. Horn of Roncevalles. Hero calls aid of waiting soldiers on horn. Tale 10.

ESCAPES AND PURSUITS

R213. Escape from home. Tale 22.

R221. Heroine's threefold flight from ball. Tale 2.

R225. Elopement. Tale 3.

R231. Obstacle flight. Atalanta type. Tales 9, 17.

R243. Fugitives aided by helpful animal. Tales 1, 4.

R257.1. Fugitives sustain selves on wild vegetables and wild fruits. Tale 1.

REFUGES AND RECAPTURE

R312.   Forest as refuge. Tales 1, 7.
R318.1.   Boy hidden under skin in order not to be seen. Tale 5.
R336.   Refuge under kettle (box). Tale 13.

S. *Unnatural Cruelty*

CRUEL RELATIVES

S10.   Cruel parents. Tale 13.
S12.   Cruel mother. Tale 22.
S31.   Cruel stepmother. Tale 2.
S34.   Cruel stepsisters. Tale 2.
S56.   Cruel son-in-law. Tale 21.

REVOLTING MURDERS AND MUTILATIONS

S112.1.   Boiling to death (in grease). Tale 18.
S113.1.   Murder by hanging. Tales 1, 4, 6.
S118.2.   Murder by cutting throat (with big knife). Tale 16.
S131.   Murder by drowning. Tales 14, 15.
S139.2.   Slain person dismembered. Tale 1.
S143.   Abandonment in forest. Tale 1.

CRUEL SACRIFICES

S222.1.   Woman promises unborn child to appease. Tale 11.
S228.   Daughter promised to monster as bride to secure flower
   she has asked for. Tale 5.
S262.   Periodic sacrifices to a monster. Tale 4.
S262.2.1.   Youths and maidens (fifteen-year-old maiden) a:
   yearly tribute to monsters. Tale 4.

ABANDONED OR MURDERED CHILDREN

S302.   Children murdered. Tales 13, 16.
S321.   Destitute parents abandon children. Tale 13.

S322.1. Father casts daughter forth. Tale 5.
S322.1.5. Boy turned out of doors by father (mother). Tale 12.
S327. Child cast out because of his stupidity. Tale 22.
S336.1. Abandoned child, well wrapped, found near well. Tale 4.

CRUEL PERSECUTIONS

S451. Outcast wife at last united with husband and children. Tale 1.
S481. Cruelty to animals. Tales 31, 33.

T. Sex

LOVE

T10. Falling in love. Tales 2, 3, 4, 5, 6, 19.
T10.1.2. Love transforms crude individual into polished courtier. Tale 12.
T11. Falling in love with person never seen. Tale 19.
T11.2. Love through sight of picture (doll). Tale 18.
T15. Love at first sight. Tale 2.
T30. Lover's meeting: hero in service of lady's father. Tale 3.
T35.0.1. Lover (husband) late at rendezvous. Tales 3, 19.
T41.1. Communication of lovers through hole in wall. Tale 19.
T66.1. Grateful dead man helps hero win princess. Tale 10.
T68. Princess offered as prize. Tale 9.
T68.1. Princess offered as prize to rescuer. Tale 6.
T75. Man scorned by his beloved. Tales 4, 6.
T75.2.1. Rejected suitor's revenge. Tale 1.
T91.3.1. Supernatural lover performs girl's work. Tale 11.
T91.5.1. Rich girl in love with poor boy. Tale 3.
T91.6. Noble and lowly in love. Tale 2.
T91.6.2. King (prince) in love with a lowly girl. Tales 2, 5.
T91.6.4. Princess falls in love with lowly boy. Tale 4.
T91.7.2. Falling in love with someone of a different caste. Tale 2.

T92.11. Rivals contesting for the same girl. Tale 9.

T96. Lovers reunited after many adventures. Tales 3, 19.

MARRIAGE

T102. Hero returns and marries first love. Tales 3, 19.

T136.1. Wedding feast. Tales 3, 4, 6, 18, 19.

T151.3. Other respites from unwelcome marriage. (Marriage not to take place for a year and a day.) Tale 4.

T210.1. Faithful wife. Tale 1.

T211.9. Excessive grief at husband's or wife's death. Tale 1.

CHASTITY AND CELIBACY

T320. Escape from undesired lover. Tales 4, 6.

T371. The boy (girl) who had never seen a woman (man). Tale 3.

CONCEPTION AND BIRTH

T550. Monstrous birth. Tale 7.

T581.2.3. Child born in dungeon. Tale 1.

T611.7. Abandoned child: milk furnished by doe. Tale 1.

U. *The Nature of Life*

U10. Justice and injustice. Tale 5.

U11.2. He who steals much is king: he who steals little is called robber. Tale 7.

U21. Justice depends on the point of view. Tales 6, 7, 24.

U30. Rights of the strong. Tales 1, 3, 6.

U60. Wealth and poverty. Tales 9, 10.

U66.1.1. Bids raised for queen's favors until she hesitates. Tale 11.

U119.3. Beautiful exterior does not make beautiful soul. Tale 5.

U135.1. Longing for accustomed food and living. Tale 1.

U138. Habit of dishonesty cannot be broken. Tales 30, 31, 33.

U150. Indifference of the miserable. Tale 16.
U210. Bad ruler, bad subject. Tale 21.
U243. Courage conquers all and impossible is made possible. Tales 14, 15, 19.

V. *Religion*

V40. Altar boys say *Bobinus bobiscum*. Tale 3.
V72. Christmas. Tale 20.
V111. Churches. Tale 4.

W. *Traits of Character*

FAVORABLE TRAITS OF CHARACTER

W10. Kindness. Tales 3, 9.
W11. Generosity. Tale 5.
W11.14. Youngest brother shares wealth with older brothers who foolishly lost theirs. Tale 10.
W12. Hospitality. Tales 9, 10.
W26. Patience. Tales 7, 20.
W27. Gratitude. Tale 10.
W28. Self-sacrifice. Tale 5.
W32. Bravery. Tales 4, 5.
W33. Heroism. Tales 6, 19.
W34. Loyalty. Tale 4.

UNFAVORABLE TRAITS OF CHARACTER

W111. Laziness. Tale 12.
W116. Vanity. Tale 2.
W137. Curiosity. Tale 6.
W151. Greed. Tale 8.
W154. Ingratitude and disloyalty. Tale 1.
W155. Hardness of heart. Tales 7, 13.
W157. Dishonesty. Tales 8, 21, 31, 33.

W158.   Inhospitality. Tale 9.
W181.   Jealousy. Tales 2, 6, 7.
W187.   Insolence. Tale 15.
W188.   Contentiousness. Tale 14.
W195.   Envy. Tale 6.
W211.   Active imagination. Tale 24.
W215.   Extreme prudence. Tale 27.

X. *Humor*

X137.   Humor of ugliness. Tale 23.
X650.   Jokes concerning other nations (Italians). Tale 28.
X750.   Jokes on old maids (bachelors). Tale 27.
X1233.3.   Lies about thin hogs. Tale 21.
X1340.   Lie: extraordinary amphibia and other animals. Tales 30, 31, 32, 33.
X1623.2.1.   Lie: frozen words thaw out in the spring. Tale 26.
X1700.   Lies: logical absurdities. Tale 22.
X1723.1.2.   Lie: man swallowed by fish and later rescued alive. Tale 28.

Z. *Miscellaneous Groups and Motifs*

CUMULATIVE TALES

Z41.   Chains with interdependent members. Tale 29.
Z51.   Chains involving contradictions or extremes. Tale 25.
Z62.1.   The old and the new keys. Tales 3, 19.
Z71.1.   Formulistic number: three. Tales 7, 9, 10, 20.
Z72.1.   A year and a day. Tale 4.

SYMBOLISM

Z174.   Message or orders given symbolic action. Tale 32.

HEROES

Z230. Extraordinary exploits of hero. ('Tit Jean is the most popular hero in southern Louisiana folklore.) Tales 17, 18, 19.

UNIQUE EXCEPTIONS

Z300. Unique exceptions.
- (*a*) Do not remove the bridle. Tale 8.
- (*b*) Do not enter room seven. Tale 6.

PUBLISHED VARIANTS
OF THE TALES

THESE VARIANTS show the origin of our tales and the effect of time and environment upon them. Some are only fragments of the original folk tales. (See also the variants printed in the text, Tales 22a, 24a–b, and 33a.)

Most of these variants are found either in Elsie Clews Parsons, *Folk-Lore of the Antilles, French and English* (published as *Memoirs of the American Folk-Lore Society*, Vol. 26, Parts I–III [1933, 1936, 1943]; cited below as "Parsons"), or in one of the several series of "Contes populaires canadiens" published in the *Journal of American Folk-Lore*, initiated by Marius Barbeau in Vol. 29 (1916) and continued in subsequent volumes by Barbeau and others (cited below as "J.A.F.").

1. GENEVIÈVE DE BRABANT. See the sources cited in the introductory note to the tale.
2. CINDERELLA. Ernest F. Haden in *Les Archives de Folklore*, Vol. 3 (1948), pp. 21–26: "La petite Centrillouse."
3. JULIE AND JULIEN. Parsons III, pp. 156–57: Tale 172J, "The Devil's Daughter and Magic Flight," from Dominica.
4. THE SEVEN-HEADED ANIMAL. J.A.F., Vol. 30 (1917), pp. 82–86: 2d series Tale 58: "Les trois frères et la bête-à-sept-têtes."
5. BEAUTY AND THE BEAST. Parsons II, pp. 179–81: Tale 99, "La belle et la bête."
6. THE TURKEY RAISER. Parsons III, pp. 174–75: Tale 183c, "Guessing a Name," from Dominica.
7. THE RISING WATER . . . J.A.F., Vol. 29 (1916), pp. 112–17: Tale 27, "Les sœurs jalouses."

8. THE MAN AND HIS SON. J.A.F., Vol. 29 (1916), pp. 87–89: Tale 17, "Les deux magiciens."

9. THE MILLIONAIRE, HIS DAUGHTER AND HER SUITORS. J.A.F. (Gustave Lanctot, "Fables, contes et formules"), Vol. 29 (1916), pp. 142–45: Tale 40, "La bête-à-sept-têtes."

10. THE MAN AND HIS THREE SONS. J.A.F., Vol. 32 (1919), pp. 112–16: 3d series Tale 84, "La princesse du Tomboso."

11. THE MILLER. J.A.F., Vol. 29 (1916), pp. 108–10: Tale 24, "Cachelot."

12. MOUSTAPHAT. J.A.F., Vol. 30 (1917), pp. 93–98: 2d series Tale 61, "Le petit teigneux."

14. ROCLORE I. J.A.F. (Gustave Lanctot, "Contes de Quebec"), Vol. 39 (1926), pp. 436–38: 5th series, "Tit Jean le Voleur."

15. ROCLORE II. Parsons III, p. 43: Tale 23ᴋ, "Contradictions," from Martinique.

16. THE LITTLE BIRD. J.A.F. (Gustave Lanctot), Vol. 44 (1931), pp. 252–55: "Le petit doigt enchanté," conté par Mme J. B. Lambert.

18. LITTLE JOHN II. J.A.F., Vol. 30 (1917), pp. 63–70: 2d series Tale 54, "Thomas-bon-chasseur." J.A.F., Vol. 29 (1916), pp. 37–41: Tale 4: "Ti-Jean et le cheval blanc." Alcée Fortier, "Louisiana Nursery Tales," *Journal of American Folk-Lore*, Vol. 2 (1889), pp. 37–40: Tale 4, "Give Me."

19. LITTLE JOHN III. J.A.F. (Gustave Lanctot), Vol. 44 (1931), pp. 250–52: "Le géant Ogron," conté par Adélard Lambert.

21. THE HUNCHBACK. Parsons III, pp. 72–73: Tale 45, "Buried Tails."

22. FOOLISH JOHN. J.A.F. (Gustave Lanctot, "Collection d'Adélard Lambert"), Vol. 36 (1923), pp. 233–35: 4th series Tale 101, "Jacquot." J.A.F. (Collection Lambert, ed. Barbeau-Daviault), Vol. 53 (1940), pp. 149–51: Tale 20, "Jean-le-Sot."

23. POT BELLY . . . Parsons III, pp. 502–3: Tale 22, "Gran Jol, Gros Vent'e, Pied Fin."

25. THE DROLL MAN. Parsons III, p. 312: Tale 328c, "Contradictions," from Martinique.

27. THE OLD BACHELOR. J.A.F. (Gustave Lanctot, "Contes de Quebec"), Vol. 39 (1926), pp. 408–10: 5th series, "Le quartier de bœuf."
29. MINETTE AND HER ROLLERS. J.A.F., Vol. 29 (1916), pp. 135–36: Tale 37, "Minette m'a volé mes roulettes."
30. BRER GOAT. J.A.F., Vol. 30 (1917), pp. 113–14: 2d series Tale 65, "La fable de l'ours et du Rénard." Parsons III, p. 95: Tale 73A, "Playing Godfather," from Trinidad.
31 and 32. BRER TURTLE. THE HUNGRY BEAR. Alcée Fortier, "Bits of Louisiana Folk-Lore," *Transactions and Proceedings of the Modern Language Association*, Vol. 3 (1887), pp. 101–68.
33. BRER RABBIT. Parsons III, pp. 19–20: Tale 8, "Shou! Shou! 'tit mouche." Joel Chandler Harris, *Nights With Uncle Remus* (Boston, 1883).

BIBLIOGRAPHY

BOOKS

Aarne, Antti, *The Types of the Folk-Tale: A Classification and Bibliography.* Translated by Stith Thompson. Folklore Fellows Communication, No. 74. Helsinki, 1928.

Botkin, B. A., *A Treasury of American Folklore.* New York, 1944.

Carriere, Joseph Medard, *Tales From the French Folklore of Missouri.* Evanston and Chicago, 1937.

Caulfield, Ruby Van Allen, *The French Literature of Louisiana.* Columbia University, New York, 1929.

Harris, Joel Chandler, *Nights With Uncle Remus: Myths and Legends of Old Plantations.* Boston, 1883.

Lee, F. H., *Folktales of All Nations.* New York 1932.

Parsons, Elsie Clews, *Folk-Lore of the Antilles, French and English,* Parts I–III. (*Memoirs of the American Folk-Lore Society,* Vol. 26, Parts I–III.) New York, 1933, 1936, 1943.

Perrault, Charles, *Contes.* Les Éditions Variétés, Montreal, 1946.

Saint-Ives, Paul, *Manuel de Folklore.* Paris, 1936.

Saucier, Corinne L., *Traditions de la paroisse des Avoyelles en Louisiane. (Memoirs of the American Folk-Lore Society,* Vol. 47.) Philadelphia, 1956.

Sébillot, Paul, *Le folklore de France,* 4 vols. Librairie Orientale et Américane, Paris, 1904.

Thompson, Stith, *Motif-Index of Folk-Literature: A Classification of Narrative Elements in Folktales, Ballads, Myths, Fables, Mediaeval Romances, Exempla, Fabliaux, Jest-Books, and Local Legends,* 6 vols. Rev. and enl. ed. Indiana University Press, Bloomington, 1955–57.

—— *The Folktale.* New York, 1946.

THESES

Bordelon, Marjorie, "A Study of a Rural Town in Louisiana—Cottonport, Avoyelles Parish." Master's Thesis, Tulane University, New Orleans, Louisiana, 1936.

Claudel, Calvin A., "A Study of Louisiana French Folktales in Avoyelles Parish." Dissertation, University of North Carolina, Chapel Hill, North Carolina, 1948.

Dunn, Velmarae, "A Study of the Louisiana Acadians as They Are Reflected in the Fiction of Louisiana." Master's Thesis, Oklahoma, 1937.

Saucier, Corinne L., "Louisiana Folk-tales and Songs in French Dialect, With Linguistic Notes." Master's Thesis, Peabody, 1923.

Stone, Ophelia, "Ruth McEnery Stuart in Dialect and Folklore." Master's Thesis, Columbia, 1922.

Wagner, Irene C., "A Study of the Folklore of Louisiana, With Special Reference to Its Distinctive Qualities." Master's Thesis, Kansas University, Lawrence, Kansas, 1933.

PERIODICALS

Archives de Folklores, Les (ed. Luc Lacourcière; Publications de l'Université Laval; Éditions Fides, Montreal), Vols. 1–6 (1946–51).

Barbeau, Marius, and E. Z. Massicotte, "Contes populaires canadiens." *Journal of American Folk-Lore,* Vols. 29 (1916), 30 (1917), 32 (1919)—and subsequently under other folklorists.

Claudel, Calvin A., "History of the Louisiana Folklore Association." *Southern Folklore Quarterly,* Vol. 8, No. 1 (March, 1944), pp. 11–21.

Claudel, Calvin A., and Joseph M. Carriere, "Snow Bella: A Tale From the French Folklore of Louisiana." *Southern Folklore Quarterly,* No. 6 (September, 1942), pp. 153–62.

Fortier, Alcée, "Bits of Louisiana Folk-Lore." *Transactions and Proceedings of the Modern Language Association of America,* Vol. 3 (1887), pp. 101–68.

— "Four Louisiana Folk-Tales." *Journal of American Folk-Lore*, Vol. 19 (1906), pp. 123–26.

— "Louisiana Nursery Tales." *Journal of American Folk-Lore*, Vol. 1 (1888), pp. 140–45, and Vol. 2 (1889), pp. 36–40.

Lafargue, André, "Louisiana Linguistic and Folklore Background." *Louisiana Historical Quarterly*, Vol. 24, No. 3 (July, 1941).

Moore, Arthur K., "Specimens of the Folktales From Some Antebellum Newspapers of Louisiana." *Louisiana Historical Quarterly* (New Orleans), Vol. 32 (1949), pp. 723–58.

Saucier, Corinne L., "A Historical Sketch of the Acadians." *Louisiana Historical Quarterly*, Vol. 34, No. 2 (April, 1951).

OTHER OF DR. SAUCIER'S WORKS

"Anthology of Louisiana-French Literature." Bound typescript, Northwestern State College library, Natchitoches, 323 pages.

"Bullard Sisters, The," "The Hertzog Sisters," "Mother Hyacinth," "Agnes Morris," and "Roberta Aiken Newell." In *Pioneer Women Teachers of Louisiana*, compiled by Grace Bordelon Agate, Ph.D. Alpha Chapter, Epsilon Organization, Delta Kappa Gamma, Lafayette, La., 1954. There is also a sixth sketch, "Dean Varnado," prepared for a future edition.

"Foreign Languages at 'The Normal': An Historical Sketch." *Louisiana Schools*, Vol. 27, No. 9 (May, 1950), pp. 14, 15, 26–33. Valuable for the biographical sketches of all who taught in that department.

Histoire et géographie des Avoyelles en Louisiane. Pelican Publishing Co., New Orleans, 1956. Vol. 1 of the planned publication of her Ph.D. dissertation.

"Histoire et traditions de la paroisse des Avoyelles en Louisiane." Unpublished doctoral dissertation, Laval University, Quebec, 1949. To be published in four volumes: (1) *Histoire et geographie* . . . above, (2) *Traditions* . . . above, under "Books," (3) the present volume, and (4) a collection of folk-songs.

"Historical Sketch of the Acadians." *Louisiana Historical Quarterly*, Vol. 35 (1950), pp. 63–69.

History of Avoyelles Parish. Pelican Publishing Co., New Orleans, 1943.

"My Summer in Bogotá, Colombia." Peabody *Reflector,* August, 1940; *Modern Language Journal,* January, 1941.

"Ups and Downs of Collecting Folklore in Avoyelles Parish, The: An Informal Address to the Louisiana Folklore Society, April 19, 1958." *Louisiana Folklore Miscellany,* August, 1961, pp. 78 ff.